Cocoa and Nothing

Praise for *Cocoa and Nothing*

I love the ebb and flow of these beautiful poems – like tide pools, they collect the trinkets and colourful stones of a hyperconnected world (call it confused.com) 'that keeps disappointing' yet nevertheless manages to yield 'tiny prickly pearls' should you sift, as Herd and Sledmere do, long enough.

— **Andrew Durbin**

Cocoa and Nothing is a Quality Street of poetry, offering different literary flavours. It's also a chocolate fountain (bursting with imagery) as well as a fondue, begging for the reader to dip their own experiences in and see what comes back out. A very tasty read touching on collaborative processes and tastes.

— **Sean Wai Keung**

The fading hope of novelty melting on the tongue / the pay-off of sugar / the workaday grimness of 'Quadratisch. Praktisch. Gut' – all this and more is expressed in this jocular Ritter Sport themed collection that, like its pocket-shaped muse, has seen all and will tell all. I loved it! A generous book of poems with a flavour to sate every inclination.

— **Rebecca May Johnson**

Cocoa and Nothing

Colin Herd
Maria Sledmere

SPAM Press
Glasgow 2023

First published in 2023
by SPAM Press
All rights reserved
© Colin Herd and Maria Sledmere

www.spamzine.co.uk

Cover design by Maria Sledmere
Chocolate icon by Ainul muttaqin

ISBN: 978-1-915049-18-6

CONTENTS

Chocolate Brownie	2
Salted Caramel	4
Macadamia	6
Strawberry Yoghurt	7
Rose and Raspberry	10
Crispy Coffee	14
Pumpkin Spice	17
Gold Treasure	20
Coconut Macaroon	23
Peppermint	25
Avatarzipan	31
Buttermilk and Lemon	33
Cashew	36

Unicorn	39
Cornflakes	48
Coconut	54
Whole Milk Smarties (1)	60
Butter Biscuit	62
Dark Nougat Crème	66
Marc de Champagne	69
Rum, Raisins and Hazelnuts	71
Vanilla Chai Latte	79
Choco & Weed	82
Praline	84
Caramel Orange	90
Marzipan	92
Honey Salted Almonds	99

Olympia	104
Game Day	113
Corn Tortilla Chips	114
Alpine Milk Chocolate	116
Christmas Dream	121
Biscuits & Nuts	125
Iced Cocoa Crème	127
Eggnog Truffle	129
Buenos Días	132
Cherry & Almond	139
Lemon Wafer	142
Cocoa Mousse	150
Cocoa and Nothing	153
Nothing and Cocoa	169

Orange	177
Dark Whole Hazelnuts Amaranth	180
Heavenly Berries	183
Dark Almond and Orange	185
Vanilla Crescents	194
Nuss-splitter	195
Sesame	202
White Cinnamon Crisp	208
Cranberry Nuss	211
Gin Knusperstuck	218
61% Fine	230
Blood Orange Yoghurt	239
Dark Almond and Quinoa	241
Ovomaltine	247

Diet Plain	251
Pure	252
81% Strong	256
Tag Traum	265
Helle Freude	271
Yoghurt Smack with Crunch	275
Whole Milk Smarties (2)	276
74% Intense	278
Waffle	291
Big Love	298
Ramazzotti	302
Pink Grapefruit	303
Honey + Crisp	306
Caramel Nuts	310

55% Smooth	313
Cappuccino	325
Gipfel Glück	328
Gingerbread	334
Tiramisu	338
White Whole Hazelnuts	341
Milk Whole Hazelnuts	348
Dark Whole Hazelnuts	358
Colin Selection Box	377
Maria Selection Box	379
Mixed Selection Box	382
Acknowledgements	383
Snack Notes	386

poetry is as good as chocolate
chocolate is as good as poetry
— Bernadette Mayer

Some float off on chocolate bars
some on drink

Harmless, happy, soft of heart
— Lorine Niedecker

The square is a living, regal infant.
— Kazimir Malevich

Chocolate Brownie

Spotless emotional moment! The athleticism of shame emulation! Aluminium foil for chocolate minotaur! Embrace your inner carb! Co-dependency with Hazel is totally nuts. Melt-in-your-mouth-mordants. She's a real ice cracker. Lyrical espalier for social climbers. At the end of the gummy labyrinth, a great baking powder for raising the dead. Now you can marinate in the gelatine garden, or imagine glum orrery of planetary ganache, linked by rocky road to the underworld. Infernal marshmallow of the flesh scaffold, served by pumpkin mompreneurs. Ordering superphosphates from the dark net? Try Greed & Blame for rye grass. You are such a cute bean! Take a little ice bath in the compotier of my dreams. Then: dry off, unsneck yourself from the tiny golden door, there's a lot to get done. The Charleston of candy wrappers and so on. How does that sound? I'm excited to finally get started! O craquelure of cloud biscotti. Can't wait to hear what yous all are bringing for sure! Until then, have a fantastic weekend, enjoy the sugar moon, enjoy the sun (such a pill), and have a great Chocolate Chocolate, Chocolate Chocolate, Chocolate Chocolate Chocolate!

Salted Caramel

vanilla restaurant
visiting professor
everyone all gooey
this mini meltdown
over the done-ness of
steak and that the
only strawberries
available for dessert
come what's the opposite of
garnished by a crème caramel
probably some wiggle room
really forgotten how to
talk and relate to people

4

went over to a window
to scan a qr code
wouldn't open
this same visiting professor
accepted an invite to Warsaw
because well sausages no joke
and sat through a Ukrainian
artist talking about their situation
which he found "depressing" and
when he got to the restaurant his
host preordered vegan for everyone
that was that and he walked out
leaving the restaurant to its
onomatopoeic chewing talk
about salt and someone else

Macadamia

my only name
frilled & bundled
with fabric twists
kept ponytail nights
on the scalps of cousins
dames & daughters
salubrious
elastic girlhoods
scratching me raw
a strapless effect
in the sunlight & quietly
released at the
point of lust

Strawberry Yoghurt

Big spoon
or baby spoon?
My first yoga
with adrenaline's
additive dossiers
a bowl of glossolalia
fifteen minutes is a good snack unit
a lychee of time or limeflower
sleeping with soft little knees
I know you are but what blight am I
smothering muscle conundrum
tucked under brand name language
the stronger you are

the brawnier your iambs
revving the lax anthology
now stretch out those iambs
revolve, evolve, revolve
you can't find prana
like typing "pro-ana"
to listen for clean things
the birth names of bones
thoroughly ribcaged
remotely doing the same
callisthenics as fail stars
taking my favourite neutrons out for lunch
                              watched them
hash out how to raise a good fruit
on the welts of a field in Eden

8

fluffed in treacherous soil
"my slightly acid love
won't tolerate weeds"
Is it rude to put the womb on
the last
cycle
in the middle of downward dog
the difference is screaming
sour berries
of yesses
fresh roots
a perfect ferment
that arch in your back is
killer and cream.

Rose and Raspberry

hold the phone!
weird breeds of potato!
the tropical whopper
which comes with pineapple
and my sister says oh yeah
pineapple that's tropical
this guy starts pressing
the corner of my knee like it's
a button to recline his seat
he tries a few times
moving his fingers around
to find the right
place to press harder and recline

10

but the seat doesn't melt
all the while dream
deep vein thrombosis
pink bud in my leg
when someone asks
out of the blue
is your garment inside out
a favourite colour?
is it safe to assume
they're buying you something
we're in the air
a silver puffer jacket
hallucinating
minor injuries unit
all people walking

awkwardly like raspberries
and it's beautiful
kind of unintentionally
like a skydive into
each others pockets
apart from someone
with a plank on their hand
who loses but actually
wins (Osaka rules)
giving people lifts
laughing
into hands and the window
about how to
act when you wake
up watching

12

a movie:
deny at all costs
reluctantly concede
"resting your eyes"
and improvise
whatever you last
saw happen

Crispy Coffee

falling asleep
with the light on
worrying my cuticles like a therapist
not dressing for anything
let it all bleed
vicissitude of thirsty work, sparkles
of chest icicles
when I ride my bike, the sky gone
rainbowing
double
the same
blunting my love
putting it all into salt lock,

breaking off what crisps at the edges
like the crop of the poem cream in Keats.

Crispiness is the apex condition
of anything edible, anyone could tell you
cindering in the darkling kink
of sycamores
this illustrious shedding
the best I have ever done
will someone prescribe me a medication
that stops my inner child
shotting espressos
each time
something happens
a tricyclic spirit to salve her nausea

selective reuptake of acorns
losing my toys at the mall
I live in permanent textual limbo
the bows of my heart pulled taught
inferior vena cava, all the better to fall for

Pumpkin Spice

never wore a stole
never stole a souffle
obsessed w/ my leg
stroking stoking flushing
welcome to this novel
newly available in print
on demand and audiobook
Algebraic Mermaid Quarterback
uses a fork not to eat,
not to brush hair,
not to fish eggs
out stock
but to scratch a

point on the trapezius
unrealty
nuts about sums
kooky for bourneville
(off brand)
stratiatella
the phrase "I know sex
is good but have you tried…"
what's a word for fricasee that isn't fricasee
getting over a bad patch
if that's what you want to call it
burying head in
ground almonds a dusting
a sour fermented pancake
the safest hands ever

18

shampoo!
IT'S AN UPHILL STRUGGLE
biographer of William Bonill
nicknamed autumn
nicknamed pumpkin
nicknamed spice
and lives off praise
of their mechanical
and mental-emotional games
like teasing me like hell with
stuff that do or don't exist

Gold Treasure

I'm rococo for carbon
rubbing luxuriance of charcoal
into my stressed scalp
brushing teeth with oxidised wood
Icelandic moss and xylitol
buying enormous bulbs of garlic
smoked at that deli
where the staff are perpetually stoned
eating the brittle
rustburn of frying pans for snacks
the heartbroken char of toast crust
slapping my hands with liquid
chalk to climb walls

20

for the love of hazard
learning to be vertical
licking dust off the chalkboard
moreish swirly words
should've gone to spook school
black stains on my pea-green dress
patience is
mineral gold
formed under immense pressures
whispering infinities in my ear
if only I had a golden earring
dreamlessly sipping chocolate juleps
smelting in the alluvial region
no human should come this
close to genuine gold

bittersweet tendency
to be more than golden
a regal Selene in forest scarf
dipping my tongue in the gold grass
at golden hour, kissing your lovely mews
in the goldilocks zone
of memory's golden-leafiness
peeling me a raw conundrum
I'll have that XXL
ordering golden milk
at Rose & Grants, sugar & spice
rolling over into your arms of turmeric
and gold on your eyelids
my favourite surprise
the planet has a finite supply

22

Coconut Macaroon

I'm flagging. To the desert island
I brought with me
grape soda nail polish, diet pills
and 365 silene blue angel seeds.
I decked the extent of my depression
with tenement cornicing,
soluble vitamins and genuine human
                              understanding.
It's never enough.
You have to go far away from the original
flavour to know who you really are.
My island has seasonal wildfires and a
twilight called 'writing'.

I pay my debts to the peppermint angelfish
and the rare rare rainfall
with showers thrice.
Gas bills reel like slot machines.
Chaos is alien currency.
I build a wind farm with my panic cycles
and the island gets nicer.
The ocean hum is insatiable.
I touch flora and fauna with lilac acrylics
on 35mm film
and mail it, desiccated, to Scotland.
You should visit sometime.

Peppermint

wings abductor
made a pizza
built my own
minty useless man
pineapple olives and
jalapenos give me a P
camcorder to vhs
my arm pits
give me an E
square
what are you wearing?
really stank
wondering

give me a P etc
wtf happened
and I was like
sit over there
away from me
and someone
said they
pitied me for not
sticking more
to the theme
while I do
this said
asked
replied
yes indeed you

26

can bring
water since you already
promised to
on your last visit
embarrassed by
this weird performance
of a pedantic
customer
it's not so bad
it's not like
what I wanted
some peppermint
T some baseball
top
with the word

jazz
and the date
1990
zipped backwards
trackies
sometimes I think
I have this zip at
the bottom
of my
I get confused
heart or whatever
and out of it leaks
like a burst pipe
fondant
eucalyptus

liniment

scented

marinated

kiwi juice

the little blip

at the top of a

ponkan or dekopon

just this space between

flush and flesh

can you marinate

a leaf

a liquid

a coffee

an armpit

ibuprofen

from
machine 87%
froth
like a poem
and a secret,
that old 90s
chocolate bar
nobody
remembers
in too
many poems

Avatarzipan

Glug in the word lagoon
Living is easy, beauty is hard
on our planet of malice
You wouldn't hurt a glow-worm
You wouldn't download a land
The spine tissue of wingless females
fallen into merriment
totally soaking light
You wouldn't steal a martini
unless it was dirty
or a book by Descartes, a lightweight
who spoke of
mechanical properties of the luminous body

Let's go to San Junipero
You wouldn't steal a house key, right?
You wouldn't steal a person
then save their persona
So why would you steal a dream
and drive away with it?
Because of love
Because I was asked to do it

Buttermilk and Lemon

bronchitis & lulo
for some sickness
there's something fucked
a gremlin with the spinach
hallucinating new flavours
melon like kitkats
a jacket is a jacket
but lapels can go
anywhere
here like a widow
of cello den
w/ a nephew's
Christmas gift

which I stole
w/ mantra
entrée before encore
and never far from an
equalising yoke
first my mum was
like who bought this
milk? then take all this
food to your sister's
things from a bygone
peeling newspaper
and a short story
about a woman with
her name who gets married
adverts for elastic side boots

34

famous binder twine
O.K. Spool
and a "lighthearted"
twin set, perfect for
the holidays which is
what we're meant to be
on I'm inside a drying
persimmon acting
all holy
and percussive
and ready for
stage 4 or 5
of the drying where
I get more chewy
more glib

Cashew

blood lily poorly
burying my junior achievement
I fell for a pear-shaped receptacle,
called it mommy
cried in the orchard,
cutting my petals into reticence
crushing the lush patch to practise
                     earthen phantasy
                     worm salad of long-term
                           miseries
I have done so much for you sometimes
salt flakes catch in my secret filament
and tell me no

36

no, no, no
no, no
no
I make a
good nut butter
nervous & burnished
sucking on cloves in the drive-thru
sweetinfested with frost
I can't eat anything living
the word "no" is so calorie dense
composting the capsule shell of softself
                    aspirin and lassitude
            insolvent to pleasure
        economies of autumn
the biggest ache in the universe

burning a hole
in packets of sozzled cashews
no, no
more ash
eschews you, floriculture
of various shames collected
& arranged among car tires, lossy
insomnias of leaves
my sexual egress
in every possible scarlet-
gold-aureate-ochre-ruddy-carmine
-memory-memory

Unicorn

bouquet for my gran
called Cosmopolitanism
spend hours on twinkles
her hairdresser's fine
thanks for checking
equated fits with
hirsute and cadet
said hello you
can't keep away to the
health shop proprietor
someone who puts
stuff on and puts stuff
off I think the place

i'm most likely to sprout
is my shin
carrots in cauliflower
gratin
we got the window
boxes around to the
front of the flats
without dribbling
too much soil water
and then started
the long way
do you have scarves
gran asked
because she has her late
husband's unopened

40

gift collection gathering
well nothing because
wrapped and packaged
mostly giving when I accepted
my what do you call this warm
outer vest garment is a
Japanese make in fact
a gift of a book by an author
I didn't ask for it to be signed
warm but sheds fibres
like nobody's hobby business
donating beers and pompelos
I just discovered the
hassaku fruit
to make some

kind of statement
wondering how people
eat weetabix if not
the way I do how people
celebrate my nephew
at my brother's birthday
saying "I don't know what
to do with myself" when
the disco started because
he didn't want to dance
is how I feel at every
thing I'm ever at
which is why I just talk
buy bouquets but
about something boring

cakes usually are better the
worse they look
in the middle of the field
anyway the ones that look
too good are not that good
I became obsessed with
sumo it won't surprise
like myself compelled
closest thing to hand
slept not in the night
linlithgow-po
a video called "this cake
was a breeze to make
a little avant garde but
perfect for rainbow unicorn

theme" how long since
logged into Skype
always loved the
phrase bell peppers
my cousin's baby
obsessed with
walking just learned how
and then they got him
shoes and in the shoe shop
he staged this sit-in protest
totally refusing to walk
with these things on his
feet I got told this story
by my gran and a pic
to back it up the word

bell peppers
do I love it more than
I ever loved anyone
do I want anything?
you can't put me on the
spot like that
little incline
it's a human right not to
answer direct questions
about love read up on it
got smaller like eg the moon
sweet pepper potato sweet
mustardy president of
mucus and otters
is the ring around my eye

that won't go anything to do
w/ otters otters don't live in
sets live with strawberry
magic as I do otters sleek
hirsute could make fine cadets
make frothy strawberry
protein shake for my weetabix
Bakewell Flapjack I call everything
Bakewell flapjack flavour to
myself to make it palatable
porridge with walnuts and
blackcurrant jam
I want to decide what to have
on my digital
gravestone impress me

46

with an otter cake not
a unicorn cake
impress me with a melon bun
but I don't know
who to tell because who'll be
around when I'm 129 or
it's a depressing question
and I'll be like
I'll take the porridge
option anyway

Cornflakes

I'm a hot mess
in this version of Cornflake Girl
piano riff in my fantasy
whistling along to the
highest grossing birdsong
love is kind of crunchy
celestial alt porridge
a real slovenly hook
I'm kind of milky
microwave-warmed
such a gold pill
wearing a black silk bomber
emblazoned with *Gentle*

the middle of a poem
in medias res says
the difference between
"fabula" and "syuzhet"
doesn't make sense when
you wake up and pour poetry
on cornflakes
it's so everyday
gorgeous disorder
fred claims ice cream
is currently the only decent thing
especially the coffee variety
described as "crack"
I said pour it on your cornflakes
until you feel better

melty sugar vanilla espresso

bittersweet the word "sweeteaze"

in Tori Amos

shitting glitter

gets you drunker

the raw material of a story

my old vice is whisky

on cornflakes

peat-tongued

don't worry it's just

the chemistry of our digest ideology

honey loop

I'm dressed up in raisins

as if to be rare

cornflakes were originally invented for

50

sanatorium patients and were so popular
they were released to the wider public
even though a former patient was
selling a rival spinoff known
as "Toasties"
it's so absurd, kind of cosy
which do we prefer
I love you the most little spoon
the bigger I am, the more man I am
more emails pinned to my forehead
and pawned to the future
picturesque room with a window
rise and shine
Gloria says "get thee to a sanatorium"
in my torn white lace

I lap it up
like a puppy at beer pong
calling someone a cornflake
is to really upset or disappoint them
and the girl who never hurts you
lives in a boxset avant-garde
recently I've been in so much pain
I can't sleep so I lie awake
knowing I won't wake up
watching her arc
of developmental cataclysm
drawing z's all over my notebook
I bleed, I flake, I bet my life

zzzZZZZZZZZZZ

zzzZZZZZ

zzZZZ

Coconut

sensitivity
fluffy but sharp
measured in dpi
no idea what it
stands for
the boat of quiet
hours
by jane kenyon
the poem no
steps with a suck
every footstep
electrified
asparagus

54

doodled parkour

initiation

hockey sticks

wild broccoli

coconut soap

spears

gram all

edible bark

bejewelled bark

deep pastry intolerance

seven years now

my last two

phone snaps

blanket on line

people talk of flesh

w/ regards coconut
my mirror-bum-jeans
desert prairie interest
shoulder vantage
the wimpier side
an attendance
sheet Sofia gave me
to jot down who
was and wasn't there
is the right thing
in this situ to
detailed puppy illustration
lie ie just say
all attended
all contributed equally

56

but then if there's
concern about
anyone it won't
be followed up
penalisation sucks
make it more snappy
the language
not the sentiment
the sentiment
less snappy
destabilise papa's iceboat
but the language
more the way
the form that doesn't
work is the form to

select menu delete
sorry I called by mistake
tell me about events
that are going on
mosquitos
dazed pickpocketed id
apparently and issues
water gushes out
and you drink it
with their repellent
watched hummingbird
people actually
like you just for
never mind the
coconut shell

58

who you are
double pine insecurity
imposs to accept sometimes
there's a knack to opening
them up!
and even when
accepting it you
don't can't refuse
little gaps like
where dodgy
bits get rooted
out of potatoes w/
the end of a peeler
and tossed aside
for something

Whole Milk Smarties (1)

> This is a virtue signal:

  eat the ecstasy seed

        shoot blanks at plankton

  make an easy dawnflake tartlet

get ripped

  you've only got one shot

        in this livid dressage

grip the waves tightly

grow faster

learn all lyrics by heart

just because

sex matters: shining

a priceless surplus

you can have a rosette

Butter Biscuit

as if it wouldn't melt
imbued with the idea of biting

I might take the day off work
to watch myself breathe

amethyst ghost-shapes
on the bone of your shoulders

nothing is broken
you're getting better

the boy who loved corn
will be famous forever

Sarah says take sick
leave while it still exists

more pepsinated hiccups
not sure if this is torture

or a real "event"
in the id of things

separating words
from raisins

with Olympian strain
getting to first base

training as a milkmaid
to clarify everything

when someone says
"that's just the way

the cookie crumbles"
I feel unreasonable

empathy with the cookie
wanting to be a whole thing

chewing on my scallop-
edged poem

irreplaceable
perfect cookie

that's all, else
lucky pierre between

two of your personas
gone sugar berserk

Dark Nougat Crème

POV: everyone
on the internet is becoming
an actress screaming
at the screen of themselves
the boom-and-bust cycle of
how should I know
better than to tell
their septic plot
inedible nut
of dark academia
all mumblecore for numbers
sorry about yeast-
laced novellas, goth sonnets

66

simp lyrics
for my siblings
high moon in math
my rising dramatic
monologues on dissolute passion
of fan cultures
am I misunderstanding
for the want of more poems about
all the f's like fun, football, frisbee
and fisting
playing dead in the acid lake
awaiting my internet prince
I joined an athena swan
committee on tumblr
vibing belle-lettres

67

winning the testo crystal
feeling lucky to find you
studying numb humanism
just bought this new
slate-grey velvet suit
is it possible to unlearn
beauty to educate
I need to speak ugly
for the survival of art
gut sentences of
self-made successes
for all that's left and
long live Donna Tartt

Marc de Champagne

Is this a persona or a kind of splendour
coming upside clown on truffles
mau left the ice bag on loll's counter
and it soaked through our bills
a sloe maceration you make
the cocktail based on colour
which intensity of pink will
get you tipsy
substitute for cognac
under pansexual lighting
all that champion magic or
champignon magique
will always pay u back

for myself as a sort of pomace
from waste, the really expensive grape
whose aroma is mostly memory
a slice of appellation for
Pearly Ophelia
Lollypop Oracle
like false cigarettes
my aura in bondage
eats less crisps
for sequin distresses
Balenciaga were the first
fashion brand to leave twitter
hyperbae to your dolour
that silhouette is creepy af
I want to destroy all the shoes

Rum, Raisins and Hazelnuts

> The moon
> this year is extra flat,
> smooth and smelling strongly of bay rum.
> The sun is extra small.
>   — James Schuyler, *Other Flowers* (2011)

last night
i got these messages
people banging
jobs.ac.uk
on your windows
in the night
the meal plans
where you sleep

in the kitchen
on a chair
an arm chair
you call the dog bed
and also
your feet swell up
no circulation
seeing someone
in a hoody
gallop down the alley
disturbed by you
the raisin of the
cul de sac
friends with a fox
made a date and hazelnut

72

cake for a cook-off themed
around Angela Lansbury
with a friend of yours
on zoom who didn't
cook
and fed the fox at the door
you thought
at night, frightening
about a dream you
had where you told
Camilla yes that one
that i was starting to
i could see myself doing
hyrox
embarrass myself

truth be told
and this is
the autumn like lo-cal spray
why i think
i dreamed of
spooning
i asked
someone if they knew
what i meant
a monarch
the old one
my students laughed
@ this but then asked
for reading to be put up
who died

74

i'm not proud
to get her off to sleep
sleep like a meal deal
£3 sleep, £3.50 sleep
get so confused
because she said
she found it hard
unless someone
don't wear this
fleece much
except to sleep
the sleeves highly
patterned
wearing awake
in your car

you like it a lot
imagined a long
walk with her, their
where is the walk
going well anywhere
arm fully around
body pressed together
as she slumbered
began to, softly
panicked into sleep
she said like two
aero caramels back
to back and i didn't
know that aero caramel
existed but it does i think

one chopped into two
could be
so I obliged fuck
knows why but it
was somehow well
i thought if
i have to my feet swell
up with a zig zag pattern
what is that a vein
you'll try to break through
a wall like people
have done
on YouTube and we should
try this you say and
show me a video of

people punching
each other's abdomens
and i say i think we do
it already and you can't
make it to the mma
because you have to be
away dealing with
a fine and I want to excuse
people from jury duty
that i don't even teach
an abuse of power like
the power to spoon
to sleep with breathing
patterns and grip

Vanilla Chai Latte

Fairy intolerance
at the back of kindergarten
after the bleep test
pining for dark matter
of my valueless assets
naturals of gorget patches
let's start a business
Daisy and I keep a
community garden
in which to grow
oversized scrunchies
of many varieties
including silk, casual

organza, fleece,
high-vis
and lolita
to run
until you can't see
your mother's opinions
bow-legged with terrible secrets
it's villain girl autumn
stronger than you
would think
a lilac milk carton
said "chai mix"
spilled into the lace pond
like a playlist of angel dusts
fawning all over the new seedlings

released this full sugar sprite
to replace true gruel, purple portal
of holiday wifi
the hart-leap well
of my inbox
I have 8627 unread emails
I used to have 17,612 unread emails
even 32,464 unread emails
in a former spring
it took so long to delete
what the world had sent
professional mimesis
cheugy apologists
we hold up
half your style

Choco & Weed

after Sylvia Legris

choco and twitch
choco and chickweed
choco and fat hen
choco and groundsel
choco and sticky willie
choco and couch grass
choco and scutch
choco and hairy bittercress
choco and dandelion
choco and oxalis
choco and creeping sorrel
choco and goosegrass

82

choco and purple shamrock

choco and viper's bugloss

choco and alcanet

choco and balsam

choco and knotweed

choco and hogweed

choco and bennet

choco and bindweed

choco and morning glory

choco and bishop's gout

choco and elder

choco and pilewort

choco and lesser celandine

choco and enchanter's nightshade

choco and cleavers

Praline

a snail larping as a hazelnut
makes a piquant gesso
of the concrete
don't eat her
until she's
cooked
or at least polished
off like a wine I want
to be finishing with anyone
decadent as French confectionary
laced with incendiary comments
and trad sonatas
avellana or maxima

what's your favourite soft drink
currently mine's Sparkling Almond
in Bonjour
the maraschino cherry
at the bottom of everything
makes me want to flirt with
the tendency of your wearing green
to call me shrub
which is relished in Cornwall
with rum, slightly acid cordial
like I can be
Hi hi
welcome to the poem
kisssweet applause
consciously naïve

these forms
of self-dismissal
disappear into my
long internal scroll
misplacing people's faces
for the algorithmic beauty of flowers
the fondant effect of prosody
at the bar Tommy couldn't
hear the reading
over the sea in their ear
I said try
dripping almond oil
on each side for seven minutes
see if it recedes
a candy wax filling

a great sweet tide
each ear one of those
Guylian seashells
what even is a praline
delicate small nut
made into paste
totally chastened
you should
specialise your search
O drunken buddleia
many small shrubs
less than 2 ft tall
are called "subshrubs"
thus surely you have "domshrubs"
or is that trees

like really fruity trees
with extra nuts
come autumn
I love when someone calls
me a bean
which was in Maybole
an offensive term for lesbian
but now it's like
popping something
out of your heartwood
very quietly
endearing
reminder that I am a person
with something inside me
worth one of several genera

in the big seed family
it's pareidolia season
growing with zany emeralds
spread myself thinner than ever
across the idea of your face
it's okay to wilt on the internet
okay to leave a silver trail
of messages left on read
on the bark of lindens
knocking on the door
of a snail like
miss you!

Caramel Orange

Hi little orange
I'm also orange
how do you feel
about being so
ordinary, really
wish I was caramel
totally totally salty
way more valuable
oozy orange juice
all over your arms
or in some
porny moment
I could be arnica

a realist muscle remedy
like diy marmalade
or even succulent orzo
a very naughty lozenge
I'll be your orange :)

Marzipan

march pain
still want to do
poet's beefcake
calendar
joke have to clarify
Paranoid Beefcakes
went to Lübeck
on my own
all pain no mond
in the first
flush green
my dad confused
olive stones

92

discarded pits
for almonds kind of
just took a bundle
and gobbed em
i wasn't as fit
as i am now though
this is my memoir
the calendar's
with a
laureate I
have on good authority
would be into the
idea can have december
I'll take any old
month but pref marz

with ryanair
st marcus earned
martyr status waiting
ticketmaster refund
gone to expired
card
and i brushed up
my higher german
on the train
gehts gut I said
a person
said to me
I think we're quorate
let's start with language
and then creative writing

how long are you in Lübeck?
and I said 2-3 days
"I curse the statues of the time
with their embarrassments,
how much more will my pain be"
Violeta Parra
and all the students
send me their gutted
results emails
I'm the gutted results
emailee I'm the
disappointment
one
and on the train
the carriage looked at me

I'd lost my mind
listening just sloshing
listerine is a language!
around where my
teeth should have been
this eucalyptol sting
of a brain that
the word aghast
and I realised she'd
asked how long until
we reach Lübeck
I said they make them
into these satisfying
curved domes like
and the mars pain

96

returned with a vengeance
in Cologne
my friend barred me
from speaking German
from conversing
he'd do the talking
just look pretty
but he didn't say that
and the rest of the
journey we ended up in Dijon
got locked out my hostel
and did night about
staying indoors
and walking the
streets

which before you ask
isn't in Germany feels unfairly
ground up crunchy mealy
soft and spawnsome
a fraudulent
tennis player
yelling "out"
every opportunity

Honey Salted Almonds

> What is more important—a diamond,
> or an almond?
> — Fanny Howe, *Saving History* (1993)

Let me tell you something salty
underneath it all
honey-salted sweet nothings
angel numbers for roadkill
always had a knack for idle talk
your insatiable ability to sleep
in any situation
I supplement with honey-
covered lozenges, wastewater

of a paste of trust
many ways to say
clarity is not the absolute
better to just understand
the taste of knowing
is hard as almonds
and diamonds
somebody emailed
last night
concerning the wrong day
perfumed with being
swindled into affinity
call me your modern woody rose
mimosa absolute
so irresistible

100

another salt rinse
when was the last time
anything literal happened
car crash childhood
watching my friends become
silver-haired and petty
with a spore vengeance
sharing glass mitochondria
in the image of a torsoless translucence
what burial do I deserve
the carrot or the schtick
lots of the same
blossoms of oil paint
all in political soup
imagine saying this

represented awakening
and hope, a slag heap
open to saplings
growing in cinders and sherries
who says this is "blanched"
to be in the outside skin of a sister
wanting simple infinity, Lemon Coke
and ocean calm
ancient misty morning cigarette
having a mote with you
meaning that dust has been in your iris
gold dollar, gold cologne
washing my honey self
in the bubble wrap winter light
can't be coming down again

ground to marzipan
blood sugar of the zero hour
transmutation
chewing my vitals
tender quintessence

Olympia

hard like a tyre
soft affections
the poem oozy
in the cold cold
yog like when it
hits the yog
in a new school
sweat shirt
I got given a gift
by a seven year old
and asked her to
give it a name
and she chose the

name "Primary School"
curling up
when sparring
this week
ki-hicked
in the head
and didn't mind
it doesn't hurt
meet me in the
transverse curbing
just these shorts
not my legs
they're a little
short all the ok
watch naked

gun honestly there's
a bit he says "bingo"
when looking for
evidence and pulls
out a bingo card
snooky lumps
transient stands
and the scratch
on my head is
high demand
for cw is in bits
is nuts let's hope they
bring their appetite
and the trainer
like am I going too hard

106

quasi mythical
will you tell me if I'm
going too hard
and I'm like oh no
I won't but yes ok
I will anyway
and my body
little here and there
a famous truce
with itself
doesn't grow on trees
does some weird
stuff like pulses
I printed off a sign-up
sheet for a pizzeria

at my gran's block
and keeping the columns
apart was a nightmare
she gave me two scarves
18 name spaces
I'm a big one for
hanging clothes on
any available lip or
ridge im sorry
my shoulders
my elbows flay
i have a thing
where two hairs
grow out each follicle
I have one shoulder

attached and one
unattached like
an unfair polyamorous
arrangement that I'm
sure works very well for
all involved
on the podcast
there's a dog called toast
someone's dog started
eating off a big communal
plate and people
got stressed
but I'd have finished off
that communal plate
pistachio the most

grass-kneed nut
I can't tell you
why I like it
a lot I want to tell
you but it sounds
stupid like it's
not that it makes
me feel tough because
most of the time
it makes me feel weak
and slow and like
my reactions are on
dialup
read into that what
you will

it's that even if I
fall or get hit badly
I know it wasn't
meant we're
actually trying
to get better
and intentions
not withstanding
my mistakes which
are frequent
my rolls really bad
my knees jangling
he reads my mind
he sees what I'm
about to do

before I do it
and tells me my
next move
like an unsauteed
sofrito uptight
someone
just tapped you
or your poems
without organs
and actually
a cryo-sauna
to stem the flow

Game Day

At the spam social someone said
nobody talks about poetry any more
so let's talk about poetry as football
and football as poetry, a beautiful game
The I is a manager, arranging everything
in unpredictable ways, turning the page
is a yellow card, caesura are fouls,
there was some disagreement as to
whether the volta was a goal or save
what's enjambement but a scoring
opportunity, the red card of cliché
rhyming offside with lyrical clinamen
determination, dedication & discipline
the penalty shootout of final couplets

Corn Tortilla Chips

the rhubarb is
poached in champagne
says a restaurant review
which feels like it lacks
crunch and triangulation
i remember playing hockey
with a ball not a puck
every day i keep predicting
less rain more bite
and the world keeps disappointing
on the 27th doing
a run on hard packed sand
my mum has a tap

for sparkling
water like a childhood
fantasy only banana
milkshake or something
actually love gloopy
forever-melted-even-when-not
non-cheese
hail drives into my face
which gets poached in a
kind of pain without
a silent g but with
something approaching
the sound "cham" when
it chips into me

Alpine Milk Chocolate

Jennifer Connelly in *Phenomena*
called Lady of the Flies
last night summoned a swarm
on the moonlit Swiss loch
on fire
all in white
always wondered if
lochs existed outside Scotland
white skirt, white shirt, white tie
her drip was fire emoji
the loch isle of hyperbole
some place you haven't been
it gives me chilblains

116

breaking off bits
of time
clunks in my muscles
she doesn't bat a lash
the others shriek
like banshees
what a waste
of energy
the valley girls
high on snow
lost myself
in the ice bath
of her eyes
I used to read
the Chalet School novels

cover to cover
a problem, genius, redheads,
feud, adrienne, trials, theadora
two sams, lavender, jo to the rescue
mary-lou and the future
another gone missing
anonymous
international
sensate curlicue
in cinema
self-mutilating
half-moons of cuticles
with the popcorn
all over the floor
royalty-free

118

feeling my organs
swoon in the
memory foam
morning the whey-
coloured Sunday
swallowing the
pregnant idea
of alpenglow
Alex said in lockdown
with rocks
she'd smash
chunks of ice
from Loch Ard
to swim in it
our extremities

shades of being
pugnacious
by twilight
a tranquillised
pink-red
crying icicles
opposite the solar disk
which is playing
the real hits like
the somnambulists
will inherit the earth

Christmas Dream

It's trash time at the cerebral cortex and tonight you will find an unexpected past encounter, a pot of dark matter worn as dazzle dust, a love affair with any coruscating single mother, a lopsided monstera, sweaty watch strap, squashed water bottle, this elegantly leaf-patterned pashmina scarf, a pile of asters, unreadable pdf, a tearful goodbye. In the lattice of your least-favourite chat client, I am trying really hard to remember being scolded for the fierce art of yuletide moodiness. Now it's all about overcooking the orange vegetable whose name I can't recall, associating it with the hardship of childhood I stab my fork in the soft wet frost, in the overgrowth of frozen water, in hunger chasm. Soon this will be dyed a deep green foam of floral oasis, all the better to prod a plastic pink flamingo – girl blow your candles out it's only going to get worthless. Capitalist patriarchy doesn't have a leg to stand on. The red plenitude is shedding. Gather up those lavish, droopy leaves, googling *why do monstera fail*, a lack of moisture in the soil ofc: many times wilted, curled or crisped, as in brandishing a Dyson Airwrap against your enemies is exhausting. So many monsters remain malnourished. We can live for 40 years or more and still be gorgeous. I'm worried this poem is toxic to cats. There is no correct way to marry a hue like fuchsia but if they ever asked you out, you'd blush in empathy. I've discarded old flecks of brown and magenta, ate up cornflower seeds all the better to flourish inside me, plastered my fingers to stop the cuticles weeping. Retrieved every glitter trace from the pained anatomy of fish. Who will clear out the fog of hell when the angels go on strike, inevitably? Who will flush elitism from the way they breathe? That'll be in the trillions, please. A freudian slip for inflation: more dollars fall in your pocket; the clients are bloody-minded. Wake up maria there's all this blood. Another rainfall is cancelled. I will never not be shocked to wake, the day is so woke. My child is fed by the financial largesse of fire and psilocybin, she sleeps in a snowflake; we live in the eaves of other people's houses. We sing with the reindeer, who bring us humble bars of star-studded chocolate, secret nuts, apoplectic tracts against guns.

Biscuits & Nuts

There's a mannequin
with a lot to answer for.
Why can't jeans ever fit?
Why are they not trying hard enough to
slip around asses and waists and hips with
generosity? My favourite thing is when
you're organically getting compliments like
"that dress is so flattering" but sometimes
I wish I was born a boy to forever wear flares
and be flat as the zinnias and cosmos pressed
between pages, a desiccated self-
preservation, begging to be torn.

Back when I volunteered in a charity shop
wrestling with the plastic torsos of last
millennia's heroin chic, I'd want a kind of belt
to centre the idea of desirable flesh, biting
my lip and crying in asbestos basements for
how cold it was, steaming the second-hand
ideas of other designers. Why do we gorge
ourselves in creamsicles of transience
to vom icicles of sunrise
and lose our narrative weight?

Iced Cocoa Crème

Dining lovingly! Who do you
want to sit beside (me)
all of this quarantine inside of
quarantine a big green field
filled with sumptuous grams
in my torment many thoughts
creamy and chocolate regrets
the trashstresses are winning
(nitro latte) (annihilates
self with dairy) better the oaten one
waiting with a giant red bow of gingham
for the cows come double shot
sugar honey iced tea the latest

summer loving enjoyment
I don't know how cost effective
could be an influence of laughter
tipping your ardent fans
just watched a man review this
measuring each block with a ruler

Eggnog Truffle

walked passed someone piercing a bubble
tea with one of those big pointy straws and
someone else said "that's risky as fuck bro"
bought a cat toy for Gizmo in a shop called
Pet Barn, and Daniel at the checkout with his
moustache said "I think this one's a
favourite" and his facial hair was a kind of
cat toy, but said "I know nothing about these
things" the checkout assistant in rebel sports
(no name badge) recommended a chip shop
in the town where my sister lives (1 hour 30
mins from the branch) in the cafe at the
Botanic Gardens there was this table next to

me and they were talking about the function
suite and the man from the table asked the
waiter if she was married and the waiter said
no she wasn't and the man said well I was
wondering if you wanted to marry me and
then we could get a discount on the
reception and the woman who the man was
with said "you'd make beautiful babies" and
the waiter awkwardly laughed and I can only
imagine foamy grimaced as she walked away
and they kept this conversation running all
through their lunch someone at a pedestrian
crossing was absolutely certain that Walt
Disney would be turning in his grave gran
made 54 Christmas cakes yearly for about 6

or 7 years to raise money for Marie Curie
told me that two of them got shipped to
Afghanistan I took a picture of my back in a
mirror in an elevator because I thought my
bum looked like a pudding

Buenos Días

together mode
pass
soup of nothing
basically numb
on teams
like 7 billion
me points
just chatting
pass
gettting along
pass
a coffee
jar of pasta

132

water
my
body weight in
dried mango
from a guy
called burns
vitamin b12
when are you next in
he said
if you're buzzing about
he said
injection
with an eye bruise
pass
holding a phone

above my chest
dazed and
vapid initiation
I'd still like to see
even if you're
not happy
soft hell of
government
smiling up at us
like Taylor Swift
ok ok
acid drear
the shoe
on the other
it's ok

it doesn't show
if I smile
but my mood
I still feel guilty
are you sure it
was me the poetry
of sea hares
head movements
wave in and out
pass
wave in and out
eating sea lettuce
the sky purple
thick enough to
coat a spoon

or spoon a
coat padd-ed-ed
with a pillow
or another coat
was Alfred boss
my friends are
coming
and I want to
make
things but
old me's back the
swaddling nougat
the ile flotante
can take you to
see a foot dr

136

cherry laces
all sorts
coconut mushroom
foam banana
fizzy bottle
fettuccine
swtr
pssion frt
jst
little bag
snake
foam pianos
jelly microwaves
choc drills
toffee surgeries

chewy job shares

fizzy stairwells

sour dummies

gummy horoscopes

tingly loan applications

pure unadulterated pink

cope cope cope

Cherry & Almond

cherry bomb
cherry hench
cherry memento
cherry melts
in cherry
blonde
cherry a
changeling
cherry glazer
cherry bonfire
cherry leather
cherry melody
tremor charm

habit for jam
cherry crush
cherry aspirin
dragging a red
chair through
gender confetti
marzipan
red meats
cherry weary
cherry wedge
almond hard
smouldering
cherry boy
blossom
cherry buzz

140

cherry loco

cherry salute

cherry silicate

popped my

cherry lost

cherry scars

heavy heavy

cherry eleven

cherry heaven

cherry says

cherry is a fist

cherry is a chilblain

cherry baby

cherry pop

cherry on top

Lemon Wafer

Anne Valayer-Coster's
gorgeous oily
thin paste
painting 'Still
Life with Mackerel',
1787, is a slick
glassy
silvery
wafer
comes from
put it on your tongue
from honey
comb

142

surface on which
the
nonchalance of
I say glassy
because of the
fucking verriere
rhymes with
takes up most
the rims all
boy you turn me
downside up
and the louche
fish sort of
buzzed looking
kinked, rouged,

a little over
being
about to be
eaten
like an ancien
regime
about to be screwed
waffle style
if you look
at the tablecloth
it's like whoosh
whipped out
brought down
a hall of mirrors
no actual plate

144

no actual platform
like no actual
poem
like your luminosity
won't save you now!
a cruet stand
cruet means earth
and this is
holding fingers
ha ha ha no
vinegar
and oil
sour and thick
like my old friend
joke joke joke

and antibac
Morrisons soap
strawberry garlanded
fish neck
orange blossom
eucalypty-pus
and glittering
the sad enticing
lemon looking
like it just sent
a first ever sext
crinkling in shame
and to in the vicinity
of what is either
a handsome brioche

ruff puff
laminated until
it doesn't know
it's born
confused.com
whether it's
a model of a dog
or a t of a dog
or a model of a t of a d
but my theory is
mainly that the little
lemon stained glass
windows, like
shoe tongues
the bottoms of

the glasses,
the verriere,
the fish skin
and the mack-eyes
afford a glimpse all
together
into this future
where Marie Antoinette
somehow
is the only royal
this next word!
personage who
actually survives
runs a cookery
show called

peaches and grapes
after a painting by
Anne Valayer-Coster
w/o much
actual cooking
drinks vinegar
because is a big
fan of ACV as
btw am I
well lapsed
need to get back
into it if my tonsils
will let me

Cocoa Mousse

All in mousseline
measuring myself at a certain percent
like 61 or 74
music for goblins
who exercise
getting lighter
a slime green and peach combo
sets off the spiritual perk
of iced cocktails
skyline taciturn
what's your tipple
the opposite of insensate
don't be ashamed

150

poem melting
bling liqueur
a pixel cress
someone in London
asks "are you Florence"
"not at this celsius"
a new gamine haircut becomes me
hugged by the garbage patch
glossy compressed
ghost wrangler
patched by my shadow self
like the train in front of us struck a deer
before Darlington
wuthering
a froth hour

all the more to hold
tiny prickly pearls
of vespertine
our breath
served chilled

Cocoa and Nothing

The glaziery of this earth
get infinity grants for their work
of perfect repair

        .

          .

            .

Like saying doctor doctor
my windows won't open
I can't breathe anymore air

        . . .

Languishing in confected etcetera

Regurgitated employment plans,
emotional flax seed
panoramas of commoning form,
a too-small money.
Overuse of the word dehiscence.
A new moon throbs in this optical nerve
more lossy cortisol, it's morning
and the world the size of a world is frozen
with you inside it
waiting to be shaken up
breaking the bar of *Cocoa and Nothing*

154

on your commute to the factory
where even the sparrows are loving
their feathers decorous with liquorice
strung from edible laces

ready to begin again designing
                        the same dream

in the workshop
I want to share this piece of my life
with your sweet tooth,
say our pain is negated
and all freeze-framed by the name
of our favourite treat
I should cocoa

You should know

        .   .   .

By glow of gymnasium
alight from the idea of a car
polishing my eyeballs on the illustrious
torsos of blondes
I want to begin again
the girl I was swimming towards
always thrashing myself wrong
and in stomach water
we are double or nothing
many baroque pornographies

doing pullups for apocalypse

my anger was a hardness I had to shelter
at bus stops, and in my bedroom

I witnessed the collapse of every system
under solar envy, cheating life
an open-source potion
of coltan
with chemicals and clover
it's all over

.

.

.

Cocoa or nothing, the comment section
of new-born echolalia
mothering paraesthesia
cherished by the hum of
embarrassed bumblebees
I never thought we'd fall
for the pristine technology of frost
proctalgia fugax
calling it consumer behaviour

green goddess dressing
will suffice my wounds

. . . .

158

If I don't make my daddy anything
then he will suffer
fairy digitalis
militant drowsiness at the hands of failures

.

..

...

The pipes freeze
into petulance. I've got nothing.
It makes total sense.
People have called me a vitreous broad.
And their names in the street
                             are an oneiromancy
conditioned by oils of aniseed, safflower
                                 and cheerleading.

They have paid rent for enormous windows
all the better to freeze inside
lush tenements.
I was in flux, first
phlox, autumn
deliria for muzak.
I decided to not watch the cut scene
with the actress convincing us
to take her short life
because of this detox

Daylight don't mean anything to me.
.
..
...

160

I'm my own articulate intelligence

fasting for kinship with beetles

Addicted to dark like a smokable crystal,
something popped in my jaw, your voice.
....
I have a number for the cherub truffles

the icicles purloined of your mentions

the savage carelessness of unlovers

give me that party smile

161

a very strong reverie
. . . .
those who keep chocolate in the fridge are
temporally retentive
. . . .
note on my phone says 'never look back'
I registered for the cold alert service

cheap instant coffee, minus degrees

[...]

How much to extrapolate my heart
from the climate of fear
eating its earlier problem,

162

that of the polar alimony

A florist with a trillion heart emojis set
                                    in ice cubes
encased in jewellery trays
selling herself short.

. . .

Unwrap the amethyst cellophane.
What do you find inside it?
The finitude of candy amasses blisses
but will not fill the void.
I gave up sugar for the hope of this
sugar organ

called momentum.
Boxes of compliment.
I just kept finding it
falling from me at the last minute
typing a hummingbird
away from mum,
I was trying to speak miracles
weren't you?

.

.

.

The cocoa of the impossible part
a clarified hour

164

energy price cap

my love for your poems is greater

than Jupiter

what commodity

shone in zooming

this close to our facetime

I said isn't it lucky

we've got each other

arrhythmia of memory

breaking off this last

block for you: a

chocolate Colin

a lot of coffee

to locomote

from one end

of the poem
to the other

A taste test
for moulting
at the exquisite point
in multiples of lilies
our skincare marathon
did you want this
soylent entropy
except the clover
grows here
and here
in buttermilks
and abundance

everything good
I learned about
poetry I learned
from sleeping
in the snow globe
of your signature
cocoa and nothing
my secret kittens
of sleeplessness
tiny burst nerves
on the back of
my hands
thank you
a new weather
called slovenly

water, we're
given to live
a moveable
orange juice
assets of pixels
your image
has frozen
into influence
let's shake on it

Nothing and Cocoa

this kind and funny
7 year old gave us all
gifts and had a reason
for each one: this is for
you because you're funny
this is for you because
you're wonderful
this is for you because
you're funny and wonderful
was mine and someone
oh someone someone someone
says run out of adjectives huh
but I'd taken this like a

real goldilocks verdict
or magimix
on my character and someone
else Japan is so much less
fun without you in it
and someone else I miss you
and someone else I love
that we met and someone
else I like your personality. a lot.
and idk you get the picture
oh yeah my tutor was a dream
I constantly crave
validation like a monster
it bears repeating
like calamagrostis waldenbuch

surprisingly effective as an
informal screen
I keep chocolate in the
freezer?! please diagnose
all chugging no burst
all of this good feeling
sitting in my car
pipes burst in my flat
carpet mouldy af and damp
I can't work out if still dripping
just like you can't return to put
your clothes on in an onsen
little film of moist everywhere
heating turned up full blast
about to do a 10k run in Falkirk

unsure beyond belief like
beyond meat
what to say or do unsure if
I'm going to try my best my gift
was a figurine of
a shark cat or cat shark
from a gachapon and I called
them Hassakku and
the seven year old
called her squid
Primary School did I
mention that somewhere
like my answer to vodka
which I don't drink or
limoncello which I don't

172

either but I'd definitely be
more likely to
like the new belle and sebastian
like who is for shakira strike icon
poetry as museum of everyday life
as museum of everyday
poetry as museum just feeling
pretty alone like a poem about
about nothing and cocoa and missing
everyone I've ever met and also myself
and chocolate from the past
a packet of chocolate called
meltykiss and the sleep
ones and fizzy sweets
called fettuccine crisps enrobed

in chocolate that I can't eat
because they're a gift
and Tokyo bananas which I keep
giving people and I don't know
what they are I reckon I have a uti
probs suck at writing I'm so lonely
poems but doesn't everybody
it's a right of passage from loner
to exhibitionist but here's
something that will blow your
mind if you don't have one
it's only 180 degrees to another
word and this is a parody
I'm not alone I just feel
you said thanks for tipping

174

my Uber driver and I was
like how did you know
and you said she emailed
you with all these travel tips
after your ride and
like loneliness is part of chocolate
see and defence mechanisms
and death by chocolate!
and mood swings and answer
phone and miley's flowers
and it's practically my name
so if the shoe fits but that
isn't Goldilocks and isn't set in
I WANT A MARBLE BLOUSE
Walden-brb we want our book

on a pedestal a chocolate fucking
pedestal or nothing!
square and chilled like a frozen
chocolate burst pipe where the
pipe is also made out of
chocolate but we know
we can't have everything or
practically anything so we
wouldn't be here if we were
and ultimately inside the
chocolate pipe on the melding
of it or whatever like a pelvic
floor it could say being liked
is a piece of pie and being loved
is a whole other sweater

176

Orange

combination personality
going transparent
like text behind paywall
if you get too close
the orange runs out
an unlike science
juiceless and lurid
who is reading all this
prosy expanse
rouging aporia in the morgue
I am become a series of bite-
sized energies
sanguinarily

lapsed from essence
my flesh segments
citrus the range
a star-nosed mole on your forearm
stria stria stria
eating speedily
strung between beech trees
recycling myself to
waxen arousal
warm in your branches
easy peeler
sap-nerved
hardly a squirt
envying the cronyism of evergreens
salubrious lover of even vinegar

178

bossing with cellulose wings
what now the dusksoft
skyline winterised
my little husk
spits its jelly
a piece
full of
tinsel + molly
erotic distress
born again cryolite
forage the noughties
I litter the streets
my orange adores me

Dark Whole Hazelnuts Amaranth

Sumptuous and lousy as a mermaid
selling their tears on eBay, baleful
and dark whole motions of sea weep
hibernate with crystals
when a mummy and daddy
live action roleplays the mega pulsar
at the bottom of the ocean love-
lies-bleeding balloon crustacean
protein-stuffed to burst in
a demigod's sugar gums some
kind of polyamorous flower is
deciding to be a troglodyte
in the sixteenth century

180

feeling of the long blonde
kelp effect
seamstresses working
overtime to perfect illusions
nicotinic
clicking stitches in the seabeds
of fuck boys, their unquenchable
shell games, chlorine tongues
buoyant in the acids of plankton
all that is solid turns into vape pods
don't exhale for it will
break the game away
swallowing trillions of lifeforms
as if you could save them, puny
auroras spilling from your porcelain name

a pseudocyesis of the superocean
amaranth, amaranth
briny in the soft black hole
that is vomiting catkins
in mint condition
amorous
as in violets
lost mary

Heavenly Berries

The lotus eaters are living in Lanarkshire
a place like "shhhh" in the middle
of the first frost, afflicted with meta-data
and the ballad of the black forest gateau
with serenely vegan naivety
they may safely graze
in this cemetery, paying debts
to the middle of winter's preserve
we can't refreeze.
It's zero degrees
on earth as it is in heavenly
varieties of raspberry: polka, tulameen,
malling jewel, autumn bliss, all gold,

caroline, himbo top™, ruby beauty
berries of all genders
require good trellises
early-mid-red-to-gold in vigour
carnal in the ripening time
of the harvest thereafter
place a little kirsch cream
to secure your crush

184

Dark Almond and Orange

I didn't mean to send
that ha ha
Upward Politician
Toploaded Tongue
Top for Top
I saw a sign and
Straight Tea
and we cannot
guide people
who separate
it was going to be
a list of weird yoga
poses because I just

did hot yoga class
and someone yelled
why do I always have to
go next to the fucking
air fryer? a friend of
mine their pet
died
and another friend
got me on bumble
ffs and I finally
listened to their
novel manuscript
as pdf 1.5 speed
and why did it
take me so long

186

their book is beautiful
they thought
my bumble profile
was really stupid
but I was like
thanks for the input
I got the sweetest
voicemail
it just said hassaku
how are you?
anyone I meet
I put
"quickest way to my heart"
Ritter Sport
as one of the Qs

my about me is
a list of my
enthusiasms
like frangipane,
Frank O'Hara,
French cinema,
friend said
I had to be more honest
and let them into
my world whoever
them is and she read
me an example of
someone who
enjoyed hugs
and long walks

188

beachcombing
so I chose
another question
"my personal hell"
a lot of their questions
aren't questions have
you noticed and
put "being hugged
by someone who
"enjoys hugs"'
and I was like
that is actually
me so there
and also
if they can't

match up my love
of frangipane
with the general
character trait
of frangibility
then they can
do one
whatever one is
and we ordered
pizza from a place
called Gordon
Ramsay's Street
Pizza which I
thought was a euphemism
for vomit but it was

190

good pizza
and they put rosemary
and chilli on the pineapple
someone invited me to
eat cod's sperm
like cod's roe
I once made
a cake where you
blitz the whole
orange
must be a better
word
pith, skin, seeds
and all and mix
with an almond batter

and it was good
and I was going
to put this on my
bio dialling down
on almond
but then I thought it
made me sound too
mumsy like my brother
who makes
almond croissants
and pains au raisin
as a matter of course
I might make this
orange thing
with chocolate

192

and see how that
turns out
matching
the whole idea of
matching
my friend also thought my
pics were bad
too alone in them all
she said put some
friends in them
and I looked
through my phone
for a lifetime

Vanilla Crescents

Turn myself self into living neutrality
in this lucky camisole, in the ice palace
now a crescent-shaped sensation of eternity
unlovely [...] scrawled in the walls more heroism
being a good sport is a full-time profession
like playing electrical all of this mischief

Nuss-splitter

spicy hey diddle
sampledelia or
plunderphonics
of chocolatiere
all I can think of
is someone with
an axe chopping
massive nuts
in a forest
the Nissan Prairie
chair poem
he / him who suddenly
noticed me leaning

I'm not being funny
but you already knew
my tendencies
and you sat with me
a few weeks ago
shivering underneath
you
kept warming up
my legs against the
carpet ready to
off like a goat
or like your hot yoga
instructor correction
instructor of hot yoga
when he asked you to

196

generate some energy
for your face
well here's me generating
energy for your
Ahem
and this lean is a pose
a difficult-ish pose
tbh and I felt that
you liked it
my core
hanging on for dear
life hoping
for muscle spasms
the class that you show
off to didn't notice

they didn't notice but still
you told them
like a show off
can they smell
boxing liniment
the carpet is more
energetic than
you will ever be
still is motion
rest is mystery
boxing liniment
pervades
my legs
gummy leaning
hotter than yoga

198

hotter than pose
I have a speaker
on my seat
all of my speaking
is done inside
splitter wood chopper
arranged in piles
my head first
all of my poems
exist never in
books suck
the life out of
me
videos of
terrified honey

badgers f2f
with swooping
owls
stories that
cheer you up
Lula wins!
halloween
what I haven't done
in a workshop
this poetry
lurk much?
one of my gyms
had a seafood
restaurant move in
underneath and

200

smells of
homophonic
mussels
I don't feel
like I have different parts
of my brain

Sesame

original
glom king
elmo
lmao
bubble O
seven
forest saucy
frozen yacht
furry red
synapse
precis on
my debt to
the proteus

202

reels of
fake lyric
the frontal
lobe
errancy
more
grey hum
mush
of the
common
brain tree
clever as
candida
can't be
specific

at any

limbic

institution

such a

matriarch

trying to

loosen

utopia

on main

from a

shit salary

alacrity

xantho-

phyllia

sleigh

204

belter

that

paid

for a

bus

to

ex-

press

theory

in a flower-

like aggregate

of oxytocin

yellow-

brown

crystals

gaslit with
asterisms
doing a
flash diet
attention
seekers
oil-rich
assessed
in verse
with the
lesser
thought
cultivar
old as
trashy

206

Oscar
hiccups
on early
release

White Cinnamon Crisp

This at least is pure shit!
Swayze as verb!
not a garden!
ok for me!
fig everything!
ott on the f'ng feels!
spilt the cinnamon this time!
thought you'd burst into tears!
alright if you like neeps!
condensed milk!
get all this papaya outta here!
no business looming!
don't start!

208

a few tweaks!
mush much?!
satire unviable!
way too much time at the keyboard!
prize worthy and not in a good way!
the kind of poem i delight in loathing!
!
diary under pillow!
oh there is such a thing!
sentence screams gimme a deal!
a touch wonky!
...and anachronistic!
justly famous for your poetry readings!
a dog skating around on lino!

wouldn't get out of bed for your
penultimate line!
ha ha ha ha ha ha ha ha you had us and blew
it!

Cranberry Nuss

Sick of being typecast for the fall, serving
the immune systems of gloop economists
I've seen enough
round here to never
        grow myself again

as if there was ever a choice!
Lying in Massachusetts my marshy area
a minimally invasive life
Now suddenly that ring pulled from the
oyster mushroom is so pretty
you call it sustainable
but I call it jealousy

acts of sexual exchange, nitrous oxide
sucking in sunsets

In my laughter farm! Bimbo superfood!
Absolution!

                     Better to be jettisoned
            out in the flood poke
poverty of autumn, small succulent and sour

                shadowing the farmer who
           takes their muscadine out to the lea
              and never shares it!

                *

What's nurtured in our midst is expensive,
our fruit
sprouts from a single ovary shyly and
we're trying to produce widgets
to deal with mother nature's

WRATH

Hyphenated by vines
Irrigating sweet freezes
nutritional saturation of our red
plenitudes

the difference is perishing

cost us the poet cholesterol of form

*

Ocean Spray yields 220 billion a year
what's this in kiss time freshest
                    tart
          - - - - - - - - - - >
          soak

          my friends a solar literature

214

Do good in any season, drawn from the
trypophobia farm
          clusters of berries
flourish in horny conditions
early thirst   aversion
surgery
                              pectoral

dimensionless
parameter

     Linger   Dreams
     Zombie   When You're Gone

soft instrumentals in the soil will listen for

215

evergreen in D major
call us word hordes and we'll adore you
our life is spurious so why not come see us
                                          in spring

                        *

coy lecithins lovemake supplements
wrapped in creamy gourmet
of the culture section
knee-deep in the acid dark

calorie aneurysm

a real mouthful

216

tastes way better when the paranoia is over

let's be free

don't mind if you squash me

Gin Knusperstuck

so now we get to
the crispy pieces
always quiet
never eat recording
podcasts
all the leaves
of the maple
tata
gorse dye
face all
flush
and puffy
two people

218

said
and now me
don't drink
except
gorse flower
champagne-cum-Barleycorn
cameos
in my doorway
in a supervision
getting heated
bending my elbow
strengthening my
shinnies
about bdsm
and then

supervision
with tears
and a third
with just
conversation
play hookie!
about well
poetry and
paragraphs
and "I think of these as long lines"
stuff
ah I see so you're
writing through memory
of place but not
like oh a singular experience

220

and laughter
check your vernacular
about certain
characteristics
tone, flow, cadence
like being forthright
in one's opinions
when kissing is
out of fashion
poetry's out of
season
when poetry's something
to aspire to you know
something's fucked
always

like(ish) a
swish
spooked me
that's all
didn't need
poetry
shouldn't have
poetry
shouldn't have
been on that
panel in the first
place meant
couldn't visit
my gran
aforementioned

222

wanted to
say i said
no to the fee
see how creepy it
is you can't see anyone
there in this light
but didn't say
obvs because
and didn't say
obvs because
wanted to say i
get it bdsm is
kind of
marginalised
always

amazed
printing
from my
phone
misunderstood
gimlet
but it's
not totally
but maybe it is
idk and sometimes
oh just empty
a bag of gems
onto the stage
something underground
makes you feel

224

good
secrets
start with rye!
someone told
me of a poet
wanting to be
milked
i wonder about
feeding
issues
with food
like has anyone
noticed
recently
do all this

fucking training
crazy amounts of
it 4 hours a day
some days
and don't change
or haven't in ages
can explain that
but
ashamed to
the crispy pieces of
personality
popping
veet will honestly help
get back
the last thing I said

about poetry
which is that I
don't like poetry
my sense of myself
someone saying
if i get to 5000
i get a new batch
and don't know
what the subject
is ... 5000 of what?
batch of what?
letters on the ends of words
botanicals
sometimes think
i'm too good

at coming across
like a fan of
Jose Saramago
for my own good
and this is why my
bumble career got cut short
in my prime
you know
how doggie is a
cute way of
saying dog
fresh peel
bubbles a face mask
called monster bub
as a term o

228

endearment
and little worm
and little firework
and little squash
listening to Tigermilk
i'd like to
introduce you
to my
moonshine
bathtub poetry
so
uncrispy so
unrectified so
undistilled

61% Fine

about the rest
don't ask
my new best
word is
wretched
wretched work
wretched expectations
wretched pedestrian feelings
coarse enough
to blister lyrically
or leave early
wretched clashes
of room bookings

230

lost in brutalist stairwells forever
dark enough in the afternoon
to make headway
with fantasies
wretched bus
checking my inbox
wretched chilblains
and punctures
what's worth the cost
of deforesting all the
money trees
rain-greased
pity the infrastructure
more forwarding
and cancelling

so sorry you're
feeling wretched
I bought a ticket
too late
don't call us
the negative nancies
morbid marias
debbie downers
more of us
in the wings
in heels of blue velvet
toppling off everything
to fall in your arms
sorry lorry
sorry lorry

the apple never
fell far from the theory
I'd listen to Judee Sill
a student of angel-haired oblivion
for as long as
we still can't name the leaves
stuck to my brogues
spin me round
like it's Hogmanay
in the eighties
not that I aspire
to poetry
more
I perspire at
the thought of

whose breath
extinguishes meaning
a whole falsetto
emptied through ether
crystalline
tears in my eyes
from listening to
a young self
singing
the kissy
offkey vitamin deficiency
no poetry but in flings
kids in my street
smash glass
fireworks

234

the state
I am in
smithereens
of pumpkins
in the park
spill their guts
it's too much
back down
fold my
left leg
over my right
tried explaining
this to an
interested lecturer
fuck it

allow all cookies
look it's not just
chocolate but
the virtual
premise of
unwrapping
the pocket-
sized ecology
of how we
are seeming
so dense
a satisfying
snap of
hyperbole
in muscular

squareness
let's be un-
wretched
on the
regular
criteria
I really do
miss being
sick some
times are
excellent
very good
good
satisfactory
poor

very poor
in this
salumeria
looks middle age to me
good to have
a purpose
plagiarising
estuaries for pastries
easy surprise
myself sustainable
delete these feelings

238

Blood Orange Yoghurt

partly because I can't eat this orange
having toyed with it for days as a way
of holding your essence in my cold hands
shapeless with a sense of wanting so much
in a cold world under a cold new moon
I'm so much lesser than everyone
                    you could text
at any moment in so much pain
tripping on the blood contraction of
progesterone scrolling healer forums
falling asleep on the train ahead of you
two neat thumbprints in citrus skin
remember me the way I was

239

for easy peeler apocalypse
you'll wish you had tried even harder

Dark Almond and Quinoa

no poem no chat
the thing
that annoyed them
was the
insinuation they
don't know the meaning
of maceration
known it for quite
some time actually
well we have different
kinds of bread and
we just put them
together in the basket

gift of dusted almonds!
remember when I used
to try hard
to impress
you by writing poems
someone in class
talked about freezing
their oesophagus
by having a warm
bath followed by
an ice cold pepsi max
word to the wise
running in the rain
i think that's what i need
sugar is really bad for me

242

but I love it
makes my eyes all wonky
and this is going to
gross someone out
out there
candles that
don't fit in their sockets
feel like
they're just about to
be loaned out to the
v and a for a special show
jiggle about
jealous & snooty
think i don't need
anyone

like of a
rolling pin
tapping with
one end
or whatever
metallic smell
cigarette smell
baked some plums
in Zinfandel my friend
didn't finish and hello
rainbow quinoa
hello yoghurt
distinguishing between
main and dessert
is retrogressive af

244

not everyone does that
you know you say
he's like a pirate
pitting us against
one another to
find out who
can eat the most melon
asked someone to post
a puppy as a joke
quinoa boom-bust
this time next week
a hotel
recommended
called burts
every one of these

poems like
duvet-nchiladas
wrapped encased
i answer the phone
"thought a prune *was* a plum"
what I'm forgetting about
the damson
the greengage
the mirabelle
the sloe
is more than i know of
the spilling

Ovomaltine

You will find the relevant ingredient
in the help meringue of your browser.
Do not fear inadequate
the quarrel of your vixen
to whose coven I belong
in the oval window
I turned in fury
firing my own nerves.
~ ~ ~ ~ ~ ~ ~ ~ ~ ~ ~ ~ ~ ~ ~ ~ ~ ~

We will remember the passageways
chosen on your behalf by
men of leech, lard, premieres.
The gospel truth of commerce is

247

fungus money
swelling all over the helpless fields of
science,
Matisse, English and tectrices.
We have grown inside their arteries
a rare, renewable partyschlager
reaching true net zero by dawn.
Can't sleep?
Try it, you'll like it.
Ovomaltine — the high life!
Ovomaltine — your way!
Ovomaltine — it's like heaven!
Sexting sestinas through the wee hours
in lieu of our fasting
Cirque de la Lune of the systole

A leaner, meaner Ovomaltine
A major supplier of UK energy
A minor supplicant of the DWP
I can't make simple changes to save on bills
because I don't own my home
I can't even paint the walls
black and lavender
or call a boiler expert.
Easier to live in the software of goose egg
and eat readymix hypertext markup.
If you're going to put this much
misery in the body politic
how could you not expect these lifetimes
                    of shit to come out?
~ ~

~ ~

~ ~

I listened to Catatonia
tell me dreaming is for silicone and poetry.
Dreaming is for the moonseed
climbing all up inside me
declare your obscenity
better the gag reflex
of the dandelion.

Diet Plain

Alas, alas, alas
Petulant liquor, milk, simple syrup
poured into the hole in my jeans.

Pure

We can never get rid of it
because a ghost takes an existing
living object, puts it in the past, and
harms itself
pure and simple
ghosts have to be bigger
than existence
for this to be possible
slip inside
the crash protocol of
living worry
venal auricle
We'll always be haunted

252

laundering our ghosts
to lustre
some of my friends
alone at night
insolvent lily
stings
the ardent dust in my self-
healing network
for Elliott's tesseract
hashing reality
empty calorie
snowflakes of
pixel grizzle
never enough
not even close

very young-
looking
neatly
discarding the biolass
many bricks made
of cocoa
a house
was I once
even lisp to you
eidolon smile
a gloss of conscience
—crass satellite—
cold—strange—
moon pheromone
takes an existing

254

emotional conflict
and sleeps around it
gently the telephone

81% Strong

of stuff i know
i dont know like
Canadian Tux
my name isn't Keith!
in a viva this examiner
going bananas over
someone's gay wedding
my pee all red
from beetroot
and deliberate
dehydration
reading my mind
or my poems

academics fawning over a new
PhD student who has a chance at
funding dropping like leaves
into a zoom call giddy and delighted
just sort of
take fondness
and care
where i can
my humble opinion doesn't exist
what time do you need to collect
the kittens?
my brother had his picture up at
Tillicoultry dry ski slope
Tillicoultry is an impossible word
so the ski slope was called

fir park
you're trying to lull
me into some weird CV? thank you
for your messages i basically
just need to tattoo these
somewhere because i forget
and get too insecure ... or
coughing fit in the kitchen?
every time i get introduced
im going to wave my arms
in the shape of a cross and
shake my head with alarum
as in oh stop stop stop
but not in a modest way
with deep concern about

258

how im repped
i'm obsessed with being
liked and also i can be
a real downer sometimes
especially if they're just
reading what i myself
have sent them
this is introduced
as in to do something
which happens once
in a blue pee moon
everyone was on tenter
to see what the host
genial seeping
secretions

would say
im sorry
why i thought the solution to
missing you a lot
was to self-impose a ban
on contact with you
i don't understand ...
felt a little confused and
sad just probably lots
of different things
overwhelming me
(i don't like to
be dramatic and really
everything is good)
i act stupid like everyone and

sometimes even more
you said
sometimes i think
we're the best friends of
the world and i was like
holy fuck that's
something isn't it
so on the stairs in
cottons
so under the weather
in a balaclava
so curt in
shorts
and so so in pyjamas! i love
this pic i took

of a tree
and this other pic
i took of a building in
the distance and lots
of fucking leaves
i'm messaging with
a poet who has the
same name as me
on Instagram - same
first name
and he's been training
since 2012 apparently
and ive taken leaves out
of his book i think
he means this sweetly

262

and i mean this sweetly
and his name also
isn't Keith! and i didn't
ask his opinion about
how one goes about queering
nuptials but maybe he's got one
anyway it was so welcome
you came to the end of the run
appreciate that a lot
hence the giving you this
meal voucher
and this poem (only
giving in my mind)
which has been acting
kind of weird this week

not feeling like itself
lowering always tired
and you're not the you
all the way through
fyi you're the you for 19%
leaving the other 81%
up for grabs so just get
in touch and i'll see
if i can squeeze you in
like yuzu

Tag Traum

1. Live esoterica cultures
playing cards at the Espy
free rosy cigarettes

2. Semi-fictitious beach snow
perilous inflatable://the
bellicose hail of magenta

3. One present, one past
Speck of panic / music
To hide from the tele-
evangelist fantasy
of island candlelight

4. We can't get caught
in a souring morning ()

5. The storm of this
domestic situation
kissing in the sea
glistering sepia

&❧

6. Every day is a crime scene
for someone, a flavour of
gum called "milquetoast"

7. Counting the ovine ruminant
of your watch, lateral
somnolescent love
in a mothering universe

8. The flowers came out
of my wounds and left
to grow of their own
accord / into the night

9. Dream adherence, to hope
small z's from Lethe to
vision quest or body check
your wool count

10. Harmful London fog
blooms in the lilac blood
behind your eye / curls
that break easily ~

એ

11. Waiting for the flock
to pass / tag you're It
                  girl

12. Frequent weighing of the
damselfly, I love everything
about her
down where the valleys are

tended by moony swains

13. The expense of polishing wings
Miss Misery of the poppyseed

14. The making of unreal creams
from the world's first ferment
retelling the temporary
lucidity of savoury angels

15. In surgery all day
to learn the future spread
The Sun, The Star, The High
    Priestess
exhaling rosewaters of mist

by Vermeer, last orders
call me pastoral

Helle Freude

When I was a luminary
socially loafing all afternoon, auriferous
  with stasis
    made it hard to be anything
but a declaration of love to fans
of Cassandra
I was almond blossom in the final round
inexorably stemmed glamours for
nourishing corn-fed ponies
  a bright red ribbon
    tied in your hair
    When I was a unit of luminous flux
measuring myself by the telepathy

of songs, pressing quartz to my
    forehead
    two hands around me
    I had no choice
Dear Freud,
We live in a white
chomp taxation of cumulus
negative calligraphy
the health needs of early careerists
hitting administrative icebergs (   )
a planetary crisis of satisfaction
my corneas are so sore
    what is the mirror responsible for
set fire to it

falling asleep in your resplendent
    spreadsheet
  We have done all this research, now
    where's
the prang in our ride

,,
  a man relished the embrace of ocean
    plastics
all night long on my watch
he couldn't be quenched
into soft placidity
like a stage death, the aftermath
  laced with fresh lilacs, the like
    of which you'd never seen
washed up in New York

for iliac arteries
I was a white chocolate, foil-wrapped
    heart
with a centre of beloved cocaine
warmed by the salted, buttery light
of a primaeval iPhone
on the hot plate
dressed up in blue
swipe to exit
harmonised with our landfill
the life-giving thrill of flirtation

Yoghurt Smack with Crunch

yes okay fine sincerity
cookies for everyone!

Whole Milk Smarties (2)

writing a love poem
to someone's poetry
a Nigel Slater
cookbook w/ a recipe
for a handful of smarties
Maria I love your poetry
full stop new line
the more I read the more
I get that excited feeling
in my stomach every time
you publish something
new it's actually like
an ache to read it

and oh actually
it's ok - maybe more-than-ok -
to be cliche and basic
in a take in a
poem with smarties
in the title haven't you
learned anything

74% Intense

O the atomic
number of tungsten
aka wolfram
body-centred cubic
free element
flagrant and
moody geometries
many hard materials
alloys and steels
the metallurgy of
electron telescopes
hypoallergenic subs
for gold

278

I don't like
the attitude of
this weather
a hurricane is
a hurricane so-
called when it
reaches winds
of 74 mph
for a long time
I was frigid
for want of it
have you ever had
a hurricane turbulence
of the city inside you
hullabaloo Esther

my life a higher
lustre than
prosody
the head of English
says books are
actually powerful
in the real world
like someone could
throw one at you
watch out
what's the load
of all this
we keep getting
freedom of information requests
on trigger warnings

280

and the trigger for me is
the weight of words
in newspapers
is so light but
infinitely staining
thumbprints of
misinformation
bleeding the
pavements
all the same
I like to find
specific conditions for
crying at songs
their snowflake choruses
crying on the Kelvin Walkway

Clydeside or in Carntyne
so predictable
there is no curriculum
perfect crescent moon
for crying a new
block of chocolate
the romance of Finnieston
anonymous
in cinema, last
night we saw
Aftersun
spoiler alert
the ocean holds
one billion tonnes
of human tears

282

74% of which
are now gone
into Elf bars
vapourised
elemental stresses
of the baby gods
all that is solid
turns into dopamine
emotional molasses of
new addictions
for example
sea turtles
by-caught in fisheries
of the Pacific Garbage Patch
have a diet of up to 74%

ocean plastics
wish I could
melt myself
down to sacred cocoa
butter, mass and sugar
of recycled poetry
a tortoise called Sylvia
pop song of innocence
all over my feed
the film was so
devastating
burning my
heart retina
almost unbearably
dadcore crying

284

alone in a hotel room
shimmery Margaret Tait
swimming pool blue first kiss
winning at snooker
accidentally kooky
the best age to be
is surely eleven
genuine Scottish accent
my favourite number
Keats says a thing
of beauty is a joy
forever
Video
Home
System

memories

are textured with

such sorrow

of the dance

aye a sweet nip

living on

in the trauma rave

behind closed doors

beware the perils

of strip lights

goodbye

bye, bye

darling

poppet

so honey

286

and lonely
studying
the pros
and cons of
tungsten wedding bands
alt-metal sounds
so suspicious
many grooms admire
the durability and strength
of tungsten but
if you drop a ring
like that
it may become
permanently unwearable
so not suitable

for a man who
works with hands
here is a real
gold band
that gets you
everything
you want
all-you-can-eat
welding love's
versatility
the money
given away
by someone
on the edge
is magical

288

and scary
its loveliness increases
with something transient
bought a bar of chocolate
the size and shape
of your pocket
sentimental orange
colours of rust
on teal painted
anything
call it kin or quits
my cold resolves
this time
I grew 74% smaller
all the better

for becoming a borrower
living under the wrapper
inside which this poem
sleeps soundlessly
insulated after the storm
let's reboot the system
of just desserts with
a fine masseuse, sluices
of butterflies
stirring together
in old cocoons
all for you
and yours
and yearning

290

Waffle

edible tartan
even though there are all these meatballs
I still think I want to be in academia
I'm studying stateless societies
and how they can function
a fantasy of meeting someone
in World of Warcraft a game
I've never played and know nothing
about but somehow I
imagine this meeting on a beach
with pina coladas which probably
needs an add-on
when I had my big

swollen leg I was at my
dad's one weekend
and I wrapped some
ice in a tea towel and
then wrapped that on
my calf and the tea towel
was one that my niece and
nephew's school designed
with drawings from all the kids
and when my dad saw that
I was using the tea towel as
his word a tourniquet
he was like "bin that when
you're done with it" and
I was like I mean you could

292

wash it but he was having none
of it so I just took it home
with me and it's been handy
because I actually didn't have
one before now since I did
my midsummer flit
last year I want Ally
McCoist to describe
something I do
as majestic or to
tell me that I show
remarkable togetherness
under pressure
you know like when rice
gets cold it clumps together

I feel like my feelings
are always like that
clumped I am a big fan
of orange and mango squash
I'm terrible with dates
my little moody period
is over though thank
goodness I've never
worn a devil horns
headband those things
people say like
"Happiest when..."
well I never know
I want an abacus
or a television

294

I want to tell you something
you've never heard about
desire and love
but as I'm a cold fish
who barely defrosts
in a microwave that's
a tall order I'm warmest
and at my tenderest
and most revealed
in my poems
because I'm well aware
how reading works
Apple stores
are weird
the sound of a dishwasher

beeping

adverts are obscene

piano is overrated

delicatessens are fun to be in

my printer is jammed with

your strike zine poem

and goal celebration

dance move instructions

a waffle iron

a stroopwafel

a drizzle of syrup

waffles and thingys

Belgian for bits and pieces

ie toppings which I love

I want all possible

296

toppings without
the underneath
underneath

Big Love

best dressed at prom you won a giant
                              chocolate orange
the beginning of your downfall, falling in
love with the biggest stars in school, raking
muck in the multiverse
taking pictures for yearbook with new
                              crimped hair
purpurogenous eyeshadows
slay effect
you found a rotting apple down the side of
                              my bed
first apple since the tooth debacle
but I am no pink lady

298

cracking your orange open with aplomb
biting into my career
love owes us nothing
the bigger the better
stars in my eyes are stealing our sleep
I love the band Big Star
and the band Big Thief
let me walk you home from the ball
we'll buy the cheapest fruits of the mall

*

fruit is so risky like one cocoa orange cake
                              could ruin your life
dark sick secrets of the past are surfacing

299

Kirsten Dunst plays a pyramid scheme queen
in a sequin bikini, on tv
nothing tastes as good as being sissy feels
refusing the hardcore dark of the jocks
and their jokes
let's be outlaws, smelling of orange
your ancient eventual voice
bubble-wrapped in fool's gold apologies
over the tannoy
everything is okay
many things are hateful
someone wrote on a blog
the nature of the world
is becoming more interdisciplinary
I am learning a new method for surviving

300

strip-lit corridor knowledge
it is called nostalgia for studs
in the future lo-fi enamouring
everyone should get a different prize
                          every day
to defeat the point of prizes altogether
the biggest love of them all forever
I'm being deadly serious, where's my trophy

Ramazzotti

(food goes bad) food goes bad) (food goes bad)
(food goes bad) (food goes bad) (food goes bad)
(food goes bad) (food goes bad) (food goes bad)
(food goes bad) (food goes bad) (food goes bad)
(food goes bad) food goes bad) (food goes bad)
(food goes bad) (food goes bad) (food goes bad)
(food goes bad) (food goes bad) (food goes bad)
(food goes bad) (food goes bad) (food goes bad)
(food goes bad) (food goes bad) (food goes bad)
(food goes bad) (food goes bad) (food goes bad)
(food goes bad) (food goes bad) (food goes bad)
(food goes bad) (food goes bad) (food goes bad)
(food goes bad) (food goes bad) (food goes bad)

Pink Grapefruit

book
pink limo for
poetry workshop
on waste
like a zested
half of a
ready-to-discard
grapefruit
squeezed with welly
by someone's
arm
or even underarm
or knee

or thigh
or squeezer
or juicer
and then grated
with a micro plane
or box
or blade
or scratched with
fingers or teeth
or a car key
however extracted
I'm ready
just some pithy
language flesh
hanging on for

304

dear sweet
pink grapefruit
pink limo
life

Honey + Crisp

moody forklifts
now everyone is ill
and having babies
born so beautiful
and hair on their heads
and like bees
and it's kind of my
fault or so i feel
supposed to be
doing a skydive
but constantly
my brother in law's
brother in law

306

with a honey business
which is actually
my brother in law's
sister in blood's
that is always sold out
of honey
but they have
beeswax food
coverings and
candles and
lip salves
lotions and the
like for ailments
and afflictions
of the surface

and the mood
maybe idk ask
a truck or a crane
or a giraffe or my
sister who plys
me with tests
and zyrtek
and duro-tuss
and bananas
and lemsip
and what's this?
text message updates
about the likeliness
of the fog clearing
and messages from

her husband which
say he love love loves
her and miss miss misses
her etc which
is a kind of decongestant
and dencorub
at best she says it'll
be mid-afternoon
for your jump
and i say
ever the optimist

Caramel Nuts

Like Mitski complaining about fans
                              taking pictures
I've had enough caramel I mean cameras
                              for a lifetime
mental health is measured in the pictures
you take
up close of carnations
soft commodities
other people's sneakers
Jane says grownups wear "proper shoes"
on the picket line
mine are purple of ruined leather
what I thought was a kindness

310

sneaking around all possessive
treasuring images
stomping old haunts of unknowing
all that is solid melts into content
keep your feet off the ground and you will
always keep dreaming
my life is completely out of storage
we should be more surreptitious
I used to love collecting tickets
squirrelling away my experiences
I want a hibernation of endless motion
Jeff Mangum offering to draw
                          someone a picture
because they wanted to snap him singing
with their phone, he really did stick around

to give them
pictures of what?

55% Smooth

I have a prominent
(protruding?) tail
bone and I am good
at sit-ups but sometimes
it tears a little and it's
painful like
a piece of music
but not one you like
also a moose's antler
used in advertising
what something
a lipoma
a dj saying

happy birthday
after playing
hours and hours
and everybody
cheering every
so often
same flavoured
same flaw
huge salad
that they toss at
the table as in
mix up not throw
but this salad
was raisins
just raisins

314

ha ha ha
well maybe that's a lie
I'm talking a smidge over 1/2 raisins
but it is like throwing
vertically not horizontally
I'm a two condiment
recipe
if you're going to ring
me say hello
this tiny thing
hello tiny thing
I didn't not want to
write a poem
I just couldn't think
of any ideas mid-air

like a raisin being tossed
that's my poetic instinct
I'm a shopping list
for Bovril and Veet
I just remembered
something but
I'll tell you later
the Olympique
Lyonnais squad
are staying in
the hotel I'm in
and I can't
stop calling them
Olympique Lyonnaise
like Dijonnaise

two screens together
is confusing
my bro
emailed my gran
after
my grandad died
I learned this this evening
after my gran started
talking more loosely
than usual
the last time this
happened was with my other gran
now deceased as of 2020
and that time what she told
me was how much she was struggling

and she started crying
but this gran
it wasn't a cry for help
but more just talking
about stuff from the past
that I didn't know about
and hadn't thought about
but apparently
my bro had
and I said
"that sounds like us: I don't question
things and my brother does"
all of my poems
are a cry for help
though - make no mistake

318

about that
I wrote a piece of feedback
today that said "does beginning a sentence
with because not imply a question"?
party time
I don't want to go to
a bar with a regular sign
written over in black spray
the word liberty
or do I actually
in that weird voice
people do when they say that
I don't know I just
don't
like I'll pass on

a shop called
mister donut
nobody can know when
I'm online ok
thank you you depressed my
ass off with that bag
in the flight dream it was
John Hamm
I said this sentence to
and he was in my head because
of watching him in
Curb Your Enthusiasm
in the dream he was just there
45% John 55% Hamm I guess
or something and I was lonely

320

in that dream because the
person I secretly sort of
am in love with - it's not a secret to
him just to everyone else on the planet -
refuses to say ti amo only te quiero
and I'm like get over yourself
and he adds stuff like
para siempre and mucho
and mucho para siempre CJ
and he in the dream was saying
"You have to go now" and I was
"like ok I'll have the hump just so
you know but it's fine I'll leave
like a civilised individual" and then
I walked to the door about to open

it and he said "no buddy, you leave
from the window" and I was well
surprised I guess is one way of
putting it and he started pushing
me out the window
like pushing me out this high
storey window and I fought back
but was really powerless
like when I do a push kick
a Teep
in Muay Thai and I'm
the one who falls back
and just so you know
strictly speaking the
only bit of this that is real is

the dream stuff
and there's actually another
dream now this mysterious
person had a dream about me
in which I just vanished
and he was sad apparently
but still I said I just vanished
in your dream and in my
dream you push me
out the window
I'm no expert but...
or is it
same voice
same flaw
is there a way of

saying a pun
like colin-flaw
for coleslaw
probably not
but I used to get
called Coli-flower
at school like a
brassica and even
coca-colin which
is a fizzing mouthful
truth be told

Cappuccino

Named after the robe of
Capuchin friars, a dash
of whimsy in this
brand world of
utilitarian milkiness
the colour espresso
mixed with froth
of depression
my mother orders
without chocolate
or sans cocoa
I think it's mad
to not want

daily sprinkles
of sweet something
she sends a picture
to the family whatsapp
what's that, my
smashed nan
in a slip dress
very eighties
splayed with
bare leg poking
the toplessness
of a man in jeans
one elbow of hers
on a stack of magazines
I love the way a silver watch

slips down her arm
it's so timeless
she has this look
of like what the heck
is this man
doing near me
Kath 2022 says
when you're having a party
have a party
three hearts
looking good
like omg queen
I recognise those
red velvet curtains
live your life

Gipfel Glück

nothing is off the table
really into
designer fruit is that
bad or it's
bad but how bad
Hyuganatsu
with snowy
lemony soft
creamy peaks
a linen dress
lace topper
Hassakku with
flame patterns

328

white strawberries
red seeds
block of flats
not technically
a fruit called
grand demure
supermarket
called grandiose
supermarket called
life with "welcome to life"
printed on the wall outside
I also got into public
baths and I have to tell
you about this one
I got in where the water

was black like coffee
and it had an electrical
current running through
it and when I got in
I've said got in a lot
I didn't realise about the
current my whole
body twitched and
pulsed every muscle
shuddered and I
was like ok
now this is something
to process carefully
and then
I very quickly realised

what was going on
and started to enjoy
it and when I
got out I felt like
a mill pond
whatever one of them
is when it's at its gran's
you've got me wrong if
you think I travelate
but this relaxation
lasted only a few mins
because I then had the
torture of drying myself
and getting myself
out of the changing room

without humiliation which
I failed at by startling a
guy into dropping his
toothbrush onto
the floor right underneath
my dripping body
and I said like the Ashbery
poem with the toothbrush
on the dance floor?
and then myself dropping
maybe 12 coins on the floor
and bending over
still in the altogether
to pick them up
and put them in

332

the breast pocket
of my fleece
and I spoke to
a corporate lawyer about
this I mean her job is by the by
but she thought I'd done terribly
and I said have I told you
my ability to turn the
hypothetical
into the real? Well I can
the offer's there

Gingerbread

My insides are supposed to melt by now
leaving gumdrops and royal incentives
in a sad puddle of brandy icing.
Children poke their ideas into me
because they are perilous architects
so invested in my honey spice skin
as to ruin their own made homes.
What is a cookie-cutter family?
My presence is superfluous
in the digital city, I soak up crushes
to ferment elaborate pastillage.
What the fox said to outrun the woman.
We can eat these feelings to eat ourselves.

334

This is supposed to ease digestion, else
harden under the compromise of eggs,
sugar, flour and ginger. The biggest house
in the world contains 35.8 million calories.
That's enough to feed 17,900 adults
for a day. Children go beyond measure
which explains their taste,
training the future
biscuit architects with step-by-step
gingerbread intelligence systems.
Ian asked the baffled kid
"what's your favourite B emoji"
meaning the bee, BeReal, breast-
feed, batting eyelashes, the blood type,
beard or baby face. Weevil infestation

is a side effect of the archive, hard
to fix, the earthenware of the broken
mentality. I'm so tired, who would climb
my walls, pluck raisins from any concept
mullion? I cherish these emails from
the finance officer, cantilever
of toffee harshness, don't mind if you look
inside my fucked-up brick and mortar joy,
all the cheap fizzy dramaturgy of
human failure. I have seen people lose
their minds for cinnamon nightmares of not
the same adultery as our language
needs more calcium. Snapping my ginger
ribs, sweet pitseleh I have tried so hard
to protect your supper, your innocence

softens rent-free in the eaves of us,
nobody old lords over ecology
so ever we live in our juvenile
yuletide. My panic heart of fairy butter
meant Marxian, or the hot drunk fondant
baked into your name, an incredible
paroxysm of the house party, caused
by frost. I love you all the same
everything is edible.

Tiramisu

straighten up up ye up at em fuck it up not
up to me what's up sit up updraft uptake
upbeat pick it up pull up sun up upchuck
your socks up back me up all dressed up up a
fucking creek up to you up to us up to me
upswell upflung up steps you know who
upweft upbeat bring up up to the minute up
to speed up to date upright uptight uphill up
to all of us brushing up throw up upsy
daisies cheer up clam up upheaval foul up
gas up hands up brush up keepie uppies
bottom up it's all up up till now push up pull
me up up top upper up in your grill write up
pop up put 'em up coming up fire up up to
heaven middle finger up upmanship up to

bed upset uppercase upper class up to
nothing up to no good done up upstairs
uptick laid up stick em up power up shake up
talk up uppity-up on the up beat up save up
upland split up toss up shut up muck up
strike up not up on own up shape up upcycle
get up upload up in the air banged up locked
up back up up to my best up the road
upstairs kick up a fuss up in the ether eat it
up pack up fold up hold up wait up fess up
cough up turn up meet up settle up
upholstery look up turn your nose up do up
gaze up eyes up head up chin up split up
speak up make up blow up end up show up
something's up upgrade upsurge work up
swat up wrap up loved up all up stuff up give
up

339

340

White Whole Hazelnuts

Technically this isn't chocolate at all, but
more fool me. The coffee-soaked sponge of
you saying "I think we should make more
anthologies". Under the ersatz canopy I
meant lemon a spoonerism, belly jeans for
jelly beans the generous and many-
flavoured poems loosening their sunbelts for
more. Yeah, I think I got that, transfixed by
the phrase on the ceramic sugar-packet-
dish, "master roasting", and the shush sound
of those heavy-seeming but ergonomic
doors in the JMS Building. Enraptured by
your taxonomies of crunch I ventured into

341

the shine atrium of the institution's main facade, gliding up and down escalators to write in relative motion: what's secret about the foxy snack, a bambi canapé, something squirrelled away in the walls? Beetroot, most likely, and a sort of deliberate dehydration, to avoid being disturbed or uncomfortable or jumping around, the cause of this weird red colour, sans trip, poured concrete into a matt printing option that costs a little more, and last night I got my neck pressed in this way that made my head fizz and contort in a dizzy spasm like maybe how they dissolve the falafels in those sandwiches they do with red pepper.

342

Somatic plasticity in the queue for
Shawarma King a man tells me about the
market, more weegie history, an oaken
whisky drunk at the centre I keep getting
tagged in these tweets I don't like, tell me
could you mint beetroot as an NFT or is it
more tolerable with dill like assorted deletes
in a sweetie bag, staining your teeth with
illustrious foils a solvent name? During the
rubbing of my neck and the side of my foot
and my calf and my shoulders, the next
client kept phoning to say "are you sure it's
number 70" and "im outside a nationwide"
and "do I walk up or down from here" and
then when I was putting my outer clothes

back on the therapist went down to meet
him, "like a child" she said, and then when I
was on my way out she said "he's angry
about the address" and I said "the address is
correct, well see you next year" and paid for
the session even though I actually know I
already paid for one before (squirrelled one
away) but I have anxiety over underpaying
for stuff, and seeming like a jerk. To not call
up or forget to email like I'm a jerk for not
replying but do you ever have that feeling of
an email so beautiful you don't know how to
respond so it sits in us like a slippery
diamond and you need more callouses
before you can touch it, the way a masseuse

344

needs a combination of hard and soft skin to be good, we can't help the wounds in our mouths from words unspoken and rubbed by experts to say turn to page almond the butterscotch is still to come. She kept saying the knots were slippery – having put too much oil on – and I do this thing where I buy low sugar granola and add a table spoon of honey to it, to savour these fudgy articulations, like a blondie – a brownie made with white chocolate I guess and nuts I'm almost certain. Like forgetting the arms have muscles I'm worrying the word *chunk* from icy masonry, to sound the memory of when Bella ate masses of Cadbury Dream

345

bar and vomited but white chocolate tastes just as good thrown up. I sit in my car a lot, even when I don't have any destination or origin really. If I had a car I'd always arrive early, all the better to sit with the interval and be. I am often tempted to use the heated seat even in summer. I'd give anything for someone to give me a lift home from far away, face pressed to the window and warm; sometimes when I was small we'd drive through all the night to visit family. The word lift is a good one but a little on the nose, and my eyelid has this little purple lining just visible when I close my eyes, like those quality street The Purple

Ones, the wrappers of which suit collages, and the insides of which have hazelnuts and caramel, not to be confused with Caramac or Kalms or Calmac. Is chocolate a stimulus or luxuriant compared with valerian or the rhythms of ferries; my oxytocin delirium or going home to some sweetness is make believe.

Milk Whole Hazelnuts

Does it make any sense to think of words getting their feelings hurt, bruised and too proud, withdrawing and aching (?), because it just came to me to semi-invent the performance style Unspoken Word. Told in a stage whisper the subtext is somehow to get at the essence — truffle, vanilla, irony if you like — giving words their higher quality. I'm just out of a conversation about vaudeville, the last of a day of conversations every hour on the hour and teaching 12-2, for which I wrote a cw fiction apology short story and printed a pamphlet of it to give out to every

348

member of the class. In the post office earlier I nearly bought six new varieties of Ritter but the queue was so long, one man went to the counter and said "I'm here to post these two random boxes of shortbread to America" and the counterperson said "you gotta bag it up" like in the Geri Halliwell song 'Bag It Up' which begins *I like chocolate and controversy / He likes Fridays and bad company*. Shortbread is one of those things that people don't think they like but actually do if that makes sense or think they like but actually don't; nobody is right about it, everyone's confused. A staple food inferior to tablet itself inferior to fudge as

we all fall for, a feral pleasure, is there a long
golden bread or a medium bread a baguette
of sugar crumb aka brie and cranberry can
you tell i'm at the improv orchestra it's so
amazing, bass allure, treble bone,
unloveable octavia. Tablet isn't medicinal
per se, but I have this really gritty memory of
school bake sales where people made a
virtue of not dissolving the sugar properly
and there was also a kind of glory made of
making toffee as hard and tough as you
possibly could, and then an honour in
whether or not you could sook it enough to
get it down you, but I've always had a higher
toleration for chemical sourness than the

350

home baked, and at the picket the other day everyone looked askance at me when I said I have a suspicion of people's home baking if I'm perfectly honest. Anyone who is watching carefully their intake of foods for reasons of health, diet or performance may have this suspicion, I have shared it: you really don't know how much of anything goes in there and mysterious ingredients like "grape syrup", "crisis molasses" or "gelatine" yuck but it also reminds me of a tragic tale where a friend of mine wanted to make his grandmother's festive season more comfortable so he made edibles for her arthritis, and on Christmas Eve everyone wanted to test them before gifting them to her, so they each took one but the trouble was my friend was quite a baking amateur so they were horribly strong and his whole family were up all night sick and stoned out their minds, while the gran slept on unawares and woke to her red-eyed brethren. Funny, because I'm live writing right now with my gran, who is the one exception to my home-baking suspicions, and we've just come back from a farm shop where we had macaroni, it wasn't a macaroni farm, as far as I know, and in any case I am a purple-eyed brethren, having the faintest bruise around my eye and someone

352

said to me it makes your eyelashes stand out more, no it does. I'm in the market for an electric purple eye pencil that recreates such princely drama — maybe Urban Decay in a shade called *Psychedelic Sister* slicked in a feline eye done dead thick beneath which flutters the gold debris of specialness, someone once said to me freckles are inherently flirtatious sun blemishes of better days seen smiling ps wish I could meet your gran, bet I would love her baking. Well maybe one day, and maybe watching Netherlands play football vs USA she'll have a little snooze, or I will, and I wonder right now an intense wonder what she's dreaming

353

of, if she's dreaming, which I'll never know
unless I suggest we both keep a dream
journal for our travels coming up soon, and
if we did this then how would you suggest
we go about it, asking an expert, "asking for
a friend", or does the act of doing it start to
encourage it? It's something about the
shimmery bits before waking and it's
beneficial to have piecemeal sleep like I do,
at least for image shards or nutty bits, but
when you have long elongations of slumber
the narrative dreams play out and you can
live in whole films, their recurring arcs, their
memories rolling — better to listen to Arca
my diaries say — also keeping a habit of that

one person you want to tell your dreams to,
go tell on the dream and you'll be told
theirs, it's a mixed bag but you want to keep
filling it and you'll both be rummaging
around in a sugar rush trying to find out
what the other is *really* thinking, the trick is
to write anyhow even if it seemed you
dreamed nothing at all, you never know,
now there's a grace note. Oh that's a
plethora, I've been having this thing ongoing
about bags and how she can take more than
one and every time I stoke this my mum
cracks down by telephone saying she only
needs one bag, it's a battle of wills, and I'm
like oh screw it, take what you like, (sound

familiar?), although I do remember my sister crying once on the floor of edinburgh airport wildly discarding things from her case in front of everyone because she was over the allowance, a poetics, and my gran bought tablet to take today would you believe it, from the farm shop, in a cardboard sleeve made to look like a cracker but not the sort to open nuts with, because it is "xxx...with cranberry" season and she said I myself always find it too sweet and I nodded and said I myself too gran, I myself too, such a lie. Why must we be so demure around sugar, it seems our shame, I want to know why some of us crave it insatiably: could it

356

be a faulty relation to dopamine, the crystal
count of our happiness (but as long as you
get those thrills in the end), and to need
more and more and less every day; the
carrier bag theory of realism is how I keep
journals about journals and fred puts
molasses on porridge as their dad does and
my dad says vanilla is so dull it makes him
sick is that where I get my excess from, a
flagrant contrarian, he goes if you could only
eat three flavours of ice cream before you
die then what would you choose, it's like
how you interact with the carousel of
infinite muesli accoutrements at a
continental breakfast, revealing too much.

Dark Whole Hazelnuts

Augustus Gloop has a twitter, apparently
official, his bio is "I like chocolate. that's it
really" and I can't decide if that's based or
whole nut: there's one tweet like "Nom",
another tweet like "waffles!!!
##############", hashtags for snacks of any
number, can't tell if it's pure id or
hypersweet accelerationism, how capital
just wants us to subsist on treats and the
atrophying into bare life all crash and burn,
"AM I ALL ALONE?", the allegory of Gloop
turning into a chocolate human is what
onomatopoeia does to the romance of sense

358

itself, "something about food and I", the best tweet is just "poet" – so pure – because this whole feed is the negentropy of diet porn, to write from 100% heart melt and embrace that cocoa surfeit, coat what is rotten, as love is not a scarce resource. I just heard a football team's play described as rotten, and I had to swallow my pride, I was training and after 300 crunches (150 in the middle and 150 to alternating sides), the trainer said he'd be back in a couple of minutes and returned with two cakes he'd bought from the reception bake sale and I was like oh wow thanks very much and inwardly something else but I've eaten them

and one of them had this lavish purple icing
that stained my hands a fat deep blueberry
colour, love, while not a scarce resource,
feels like it has been overfished but that's
just a statistician's revenge maybe – for their
own lack of love ha ha ha ha ha – I just gave
a piece of feedback that said "beautiful and
sad and beautiful and sad" – I have a list of
films that I've been set by the trainer to
watch and I'll give you the titles *Kickboxer*,
Lionheart, *Double Impact*, *Blood Sport*,
Cyborg and *Hard Target*, they feel like solid
titles, crisp titles, not so sugary titles, or do
they, I mean they all have Jean Claude Van
Damme in them I think? So much haul these

days people filming their haul videos do you
think it's like orange they dye salmon with to
look fresh, the subtext of what people mean
when they say "you look glowing", when you
think of nature do you think of things which
are fresh or rotten, what if trees have stylists
and desire is a bycatch of being alive – "it's
just my instinct" – never underestimate the
motivational power of seeing someone do a
thing you love though like I might take up
trombone again after seeing improv
trombone at CCA, wish I could hit those
notes and slides – is there a special
technique you wanna get to, a savoury kinda
kick, I'm in the kitchen with my brother

who's visiting from London and he says "I accidentally had a michelin star meal the other day" and Adeel texts "how the other half live", so London, tonight we're putting four cloves of roasted garlic in hummus doing a Friday night dinner on Sunday, is that enough, when people say where are you from it takes me a whole beat to not say Mars; I've been told these days I'm more Neptune a good swimmer though totally lapsed, it's a beautiful place but not sad at all, can you believe it's December rains diamonds. Someone said to Tom Daley of all Olympians the most like a brother visiting that he must be a good swimmer and he said that's like telling a poet they must be good at writing prose or a variation on that imagine accidentally cooking something it seems possible the slide of the trombone reminds me that my sister has suggested some weird water park assault course to me as an activity we could do together which looks like the worst kind of team building fun to me but I'm not always the best judge of what I'll get amusement from, their cafe is unlikely to hold a michelin star I'm remembering getting asked last week why isn't there a canteen and I was like well there is kind of a canteen I'm wondering what you think of Tony's Chocolonely

because I like almost all chocolate even so
called "baking chocolate" or couverture but I
never enjoy Tony's and I still don't get this
big deal they make over why the bar has all
the uneven divisions and not neat uniform
segments and the naming for me is a little
cruel I mean I know already I was out for
dinner solo last night and there was a man
next to me who was also dining solo we both
had our backs against the wall and he was
reading a book and I was writing feedback
on my phone and we both ordered the same
dish the only difference between us was he
had his legs splayed very wide and I didn't I
attempted a head stand in yoga yesterday

and I came down from it and was
disparaging my own efforts and the
instructor said that was good have you ever
done that before and I said no and he said
well then and then he said *all the internal
organs enjoy being upside down* which I
have to confess I'd never given a second
thought to whether that was true or not in
all my life but I do remember an exhilarating
feeling after dangling. Looking at old photos
last night there was one where we were kids
by a slide I'm wearing flares and plaits and a
woman I don't know is holding a pamphlet
and I said who's this reading poetry and
mum laughed said she was reading the

manufacturer's instructions to assemble the slide, don't ask me why but I'm currently watching *13 Reasons Why* well the reason is a student mentioned it in a lecture as an example of recent moral panics and I was curious, it all kicks off because Justin takes an picture of Hannah on a park date, flash flash, then it goes viral around the school, and the whole show is really about the rottenness at the heart of everyone's innocence, all are complicit, on the show is an impressive guy called Tony, why is being teenage so much like the broken bits of Tony Chocolonely or a solvent kaleidoscope of hormones, maybe that's why I've got a big

366

orange bar of it in my bag, melting in the midday anxiety, what's the most shameful flavour – salted caramel – I guess a dream chef could swoop in with a lottery ticket studded with pomegranate seeds and give us a golden star after all, spooning the icing straight from nostalgia, what I really hate is parlour games but do you know what a paddling pool poem would look like? I feel like I've written a paddling pool poem but I can't be sure but I'd be up for a writing ritual of writing in a paddling pool maybe next summer we can try this, and then trampoline etc, I have a pic of me and my friend Vicki and her sister Emma and my

367

sister Sarah all on a trampoline and it's a
nice pic but I'm skulking in the background, I
also have a pic of myself crying and with the
sleeve of my oversized Kickers jumper in my
mouth, with the puppy Dayna next to me, I
was crying I remember because even though
I was the one who had laboured chipping
away at my parents to bring this puppy into
our lives, and I'd named her after a
waterskiing instructor I had, I felt that she
preferred everyone else in the family over
me except maybe my dad who ignored her
totally, you know that thing where animals
can smell fear and treat you like a plaything
accordingly well I have that in abundance all

animals smell my fear and make a mockery of it I think Tony's Chocolonely smells of fear but it doesn't make me want it, it makes me think though that if I formed a friendship with a pet now I'd have to name this pet whatever brand it was after my hot yoga instructor well anyway if I had to name a pet on the spot right now I'd probably go for Marzipan but it'd be me that'd get eaten no doubt. My trampoline career ended badly with injury after I tried to do a front flip but took a step backwards on what I thought was the trampoline but was actually air, falling straight onto my back in the astroturf of the past I like to relive it some times that

falling backwards some of my favourite
poets are big fallers, I mean they have a
tendency to fall over whether because of
drunkenness or lack of internal balance, for
instance W.S. Graham falling into the
brambles or from a roof out on the Penwith
moors, or fred spoliar falling from a pullup
bar or the many singers who walked
backwards off stages without missing a beat,
I'm not talking about falling in love from a
great height or even existentially, just
ordinary falling like when I was a child I fell
over Wordsworth's grave by accident the
beginning of my poetic career was pretty
goth but not too goth to enjoy a splash or

bounce when it comes to aesthetics, gravity isn't my limit, all poets are fallers, ballers or rollers, now I'm imagining a puppy or a kitty or ferret called Marzipan aka Zippy running circles around us, what would you call the colour of the fur some call cocoa, I loved my dog because she didn't need me to be normal, Heather Love says backwardness, feeling backward, is really queer — like the desire to reach into the lives of the past and try to save them, which is why I'm googling "famous poets that fell over" and it's all Emily Brontë chanting "Fall, leaves, fall". If I was a puppy my modus operandi would be "unwilling to be either pertinent or bemused" which is from *Meditations in an Emergency* which is an autumnal poem maybe I arrived back home this evening having actually cried in a seminar at the beauty of the final sess performances seriously they were unseasonally good queer love is did I already talk about it the beginning of my poetic career was eco ha ha ha seriously it was my first poem called "water" and it's been downhill from there like a stream wait do I understand water doesn't it go backwards a queer rain fell on my windshield and the cord in my hoodie hood has got lost like a ferret up one side and I don't know how to fix this I probably

372

need a scalpel or some tweezers or some other thing from a dr's tool bag like an amniotic hook I just got an email with the subject line, "gifts for the cigar aficionado". I wanna smoke a cigar but my tonsils hurt from humming Nirvana songs – mum says when I was a kid I crawled into a dog's basket to sleep and came out in hives – my phone goes twinkle like sleep mode – *your wind down is starting soon* – this is kosher wine, I don't like goodbyes and days gone away – so many people have died this year like my old manager, my old landlord, the famous rugby guy, my favourite poet, my friend's dad, Sleep On – when you reach out

for the idea of them, I found out in a
whatsapp that popped up earlier – I think it
was throat cancer, my brother and I both
missed the step outside Mono in sync – a
microdose abyss – Kirsty says someone cried
in her class because they didn't want it to
end, award for devastating teaching
brilliance goes to the both of you, as for this
part-timer, I forgot to buy oranges and
lemons for my student theorists – suddenly
all my friends are doing the heckle karaoke
at Star Bar, I don't really get the south side
hype, the percussive value of the word
Strathbungo, I love my own lung capacity
and the pedal piano in the song 'All My

Friends', some of them are allergic to all
nuts – I'm scared of dark chocolate because
it's just too much.

376

Colin Selection Box

Salted Caramel
Rose and Raspberry
Pumpkin Spice
Peppermint
Buttermilk and Lemon
Unicorn
Coconut
Rum, Raisins and Hazelnuts
Choco and Weed
Marzipan
Olympia
Corn Tortilla Chips
Eggnog Truffle
Buenos Días
Lemon Wafer

Nothing and Cocoa
Nuss-splitter
Sesame
White Cinnamon Crisp
Gin Knusperstuck
Dark Almond and Quinoa
81% Strong
Whole Milk Smarties (2)
Waffle
Pink Grapefruit
Honey + Crisp
55% Smooth
Gipfel Glück
Tiramisu

Maria Selection Box

Chocolate Brownie
Macadamia
Strawberry Yoghurt
Crispy Coffee
Gold Treasure
Coconut Macaroon
Avatarzipan
Cashew
Cornflakes
Whole Milk Smarties (1)
Butter Biscuit
Dark Nougat Crème
Marc de Champagne
Vanilla Chai Latte
Praline

Caramel Orange
Honey Salted Almonds
Game Day
Alpine Milk Chocolate
Christmas Dream
Biscuits & Nuts
Iced Cocoa Crème
Cherry & Almond
Cocoa Mousse
Cocoa and Nothing
Orange
Dark Whole Hazelnuts Amaranth
Heavenly Berries
Vanilla Crescents
Cranberry Nus
61% Fine
Blood Orange Yoghurt

380

Ovomaltine
Diet Plain
Pure
Tag Traum
Helle Freud
Yoghurt Smack with Crunch
74% Intense
Big Love
Ramazzotti
Caramel Nuts
Cappuccino
Gingerbread

Mixed Selection Box

White Whole Hazelnuts
Milk Whole Hazelnuts
Dark Whole Hazelnuts

Acknowledgements

Epigraphs are from Bernadette Mayer's 'Chocolate Poetry Sonnet', Lorine Niedecker's 'Some float off on chocolate bars' and Kazimir Malevich's *From Cubism and Futurism to Suprematism: The New Realism in Painting* (1916).

All titles are named after genuine and hoax flavours of Ritter Sport Chocolate.

On page 95 the lines quoted of Violeta Parra are from her poem/song 'Maldigo del alto cielo' published in *These are Not Sweet Girls: Poems by Latin American Women* Poets, edited by Marjorie Agosín (1994).

383

'Still Life with Mackerel' by Anne Vallayer-Coster is in the collection of the Kimbell Art Museum, Texas.

Colin: this book is for Andrés, *mi mejor amigo del mundo para siempre,* and Maria, who tempted me out a writing stupor with chocolate and poetry and nothing

Maria: this book is for Colin, a good sport, who is cocoa and everything

Snack Notes